IMAGES
of Aviation

Naval Air Station Norfolk

Eyes of the Fleet. A Carrier Airborne Early Warning Squadron (VAW-125) Northrop Grumman E-2D Advanced Hawkeye is pictured in flight above Naval Station Norfolk on March 20, 2014. VAW-125 was formed at Naval Air Station (NAS) Norfolk in 1968 and was the first East Coast–based carrier airborne early warning squadron to operate the new E-2D. The E-2D serves as the eyes of the US naval fleet, serving as the Navy's premier carrier-based early warning aircraft. In the distance is the Monitor-Merrimac Bridge-Tunnel, named in honor of the Civil War ironclads *Monitor* and *Merrimac* (CSS *Virginia*), which clashed in a historic battle on March 8–9, 1862, in the waters close to where the bridge-tunnel was built. The Battle of Hampton Roads marked the first time in history that two ironclads fought, and resulted in a draw. (Photograph by MC1 Ernest R. Scott, courtesy of US Navy.)

On the Cover: A Grumman F4F Wildcat Taxies onto Chambers Field at NAS Norfolk. Pictured on February 10, 1942, the Wildcat was the US Navy's premier fleet defender (fighter aircraft) at that time. (Courtesy of NARA.)

IMAGES
of Aviation

NAVAL AIR STATION NORFOLK

Mark A. Chambers

ISBN 978-1-4671-0580-4

Published by Arcadia Publishing
Charleston, South Carolina

Printed in the United States of America

Library of Congress Control Number: 2020939231

For all general information, please contact Arcadia Publishing:
Telephone 843-853-2070
Fax 843-853-0044
E-mail sales@arcadiapublishing.com
For customer service and orders:
Toll-Free 1-888-313-2665

Visit us on the Internet at www.arcadiapublishing.com

This pictorial history is dedicated to the airmen, airwomen, and workers of Naval Air Station Norfolk, whose dedication and hard work for over a century have helped make US naval aviation a thriving instrument of American power.

Contents

ACKNOWLEDGMENTS

The author would like to thank several important individuals who contributed to this fascinating pictorial history of an important component of the world's largest naval base. I would like to thank my wife, Lesa, and sons Patrick and Ryan for their constant support and patience with me during the preparation of this book.

As always, many thanks go to Holly Reed and the staff of the US National Archives at College Park, Maryland, Still Pictures Branch, for photographic support for this project. Special thanks also go to Katelyn Jenkins, acquisitions editor at Arcadia Publishing, for securing publication of this work and to Angel Prohaska, title manager at Arcadia Publishing, for her invaluable editorial assistance and fantastic support for this project.

Introduction

Throughout the 20th century and the beginning of the 21st century, Naval Air Station Norfolk, Virginia, has played a significant role in the development of American naval aviation. The roles of fleet operational feasibility flight testing, flight testing of prototype aircraft, and tactical combat flight training at this naval air station have been crucial to this development. Technological advancements in naval airpower have significantly altered military doctrine and tactics, enabling the United States to gain strategic advantages over opposing forces in wars and military conflicts. Moreover, courage, innovative spirit, and ingenuity in conducting naval flight testing at NAS Norfolk have made and continue to make the advancement of American naval aviation possible. This volume will serve as a fitting tribute to this remarkable military facility, which is a vital component of the world's largest naval base, Naval Station Norfolk.

In 1915, American aviation pioneer and one of US naval aviation's founding fathers Glenn H. Curtiss decided to relocate his primary flight training and experimental aircraft development operations from Buffalo, New York, to the more forgiving climate of Newport News, Virginia. This new aviation station became known as the Atlantic Coast Aeronautical Station. While it was originally intended to train prospective civilian pilots, in 1916, the station began training prospective military pilots for the US Army and Navy. The original core group of naval aviators to serve at Naval Air Station Hampton Roads, later NAS Norfolk, learned how to fly at the Atlantic Coast Aeronautical Station.

Naval aviators training at the station became known as the Naval Air Detachment, Curtiss Field, Newport News. They commenced training on May 19, 1917. Over the next five months, the detachment expanded to include five officers, three aviators, ten enlisted sailors, and seven seaplanes, and was renamed Naval Air Detachment, Naval Operating Base, Hampton Roads. The Naval Air Detachment pilots flew their small fleet of seaplanes over the James River to Norfolk and moored their aircraft to water stakes that had been hammered into the seabed. Canvas hangars were soon erected near the shore for protection for the aircraft. Thus, the basis for an experimental seaplane base at Norfolk was established.

The new seaplane base at Norfolk presented naval planners with several advantages. The base provided protected water that seldom froze during the winter, which was extremely advantageous for seaplane landings. The base also offered excellent anchorage points on the beach and was conveniently located near Naval Operating Base (NOB) Norfolk for the replenishment of supplies. Moreover, there was an abundance of space for expansion. The primary missions of the new experimental seaplane base were to perform anti-submarine warfare (ASW) patrols against German U-boats, conduct aviator and mechanic training, and perform fleet operational feasibility flight testing of aircraft and kite balloons. The Naval Air Detachment at Norfolk soon gained recognition as an extremely significant provider of trained naval aviators. In honor of this accomplishment, the detachment at Norfolk was designated NAS Hampton Roads, with Lt. Comdr. Patrick N.L. Bellinger commanding, on August 27, 1918.

In that year, a series of fleet operational feasibility flight tests were conducted at NAS Hampton Roads involving flight operation of the new Davis gun, a recoilless rifle intended for use against enemy submarines. Fly-offs were conducted between a Naval Aircraft Factory N-1 seaplane, a Curtiss HS-2 flying boat, and a Curtiss H-16 flying boat to determine which aircraft was best suited for Davis gun operation. Ultimately, it was found through extensive flight testing that the HS-2 presented the best aerial platform for Davis gun operation. World War I ended, however, before the Davis gun could be used in aerial anti-submarine combat.

Also in 1918, another intriguing series of fleet operational feasibility flight tests were conducted at NAS Hampton Roads involving flight operations from a sea sled, a small, high-speed motorized boat that served as the precursor to the aircraft carrier. These experiments were directed by Comdr. Henry C. Mustin and commenced with a test to determine the feasibility of launching an Army Caproni Ca. 5 Italian-built World War I bomber from a sea sled. The sea sled was intended to transport and launch a bomber closer to enemy targets. After it had bombed its target, it would return to a nearby Allied airbase, while the sea sled returned to its shore base. On November 15, 1918, high-speed trials involving the launching of the Caproni Ca. 5 bomber were conducted in the waters off Hampton Roads. It was not recorded whether the aircraft was successfully launched or not. Commander Mustin's sea sled experiment was revisited on March 7, 1919, when a Navy Curtiss N-9 landplane, flown by Lt. (jg) F.M. Johnson, was successfully launched from a sea sled, making a speed of 50 knots, in the waters off NAS Hampton Roads. While this test proved the aircraft-carrying sea sled concept, it was never used in combat because World War I had ended. Therefore, Mustin's sea sleds were used only in an offshore rescue role.

By the end of World War I, NAS Hampton Roads had grown to 167 officers, 1,227 enlisted men, and 65 aircraft. On July 12, 1921, NAS Hampton Roads was renamed NAS Norfolk, with Capt. S.H.R. Doyle serving as commander. Captain Doyle directly reported to the Bureau of Aeronautics in Washington, DC. In late July 1921, NAS Norfolk played an important role in supporting the World War I–vintage battleship bombing experiments conducted off the Virginia coast that smashed the myth of "invincibility" of the dreadnought and captured international attention. Although Brig. Gen. William "Billy" Mitchell of the US Army Air Service received much of the credit for the feat, high-ranking Navy officials already knew of the potential of the airplane in warfare and planned the event, including inviting Mitchell to participate in the trials. Aircraft based at NAS Norfolk were responsible for sinking some of the ex-German World War I warships and scored bomb hits on the remote-controlled battleship USS *Iowa* (BB-4).

In August 1921, NAS Norfolk began a series of experimental tests that resulted in the development of arresting gear for the nation's first aircraft carrier, the USS *Langley*. A dummy deck, possessing athwartship wires that were weighted down, built on a turntable that could be turned into the wind, was employed at NAS Norfolk for these tests. On August 11, 1921, NAS Norfolk pioneered carrier arresting gear when Lt. A.M. Pride taxied his Aeromarine aircraft onto the dummy deck and snared the arresting wires with the arresting gear (a hook) on his aircraft. NAS Norfolk continued to support the development of flight operations aboard the USS *Langley* by developing an aircraft catapult system for the carrier. NAS Norfolk, in the years to follow, trained the aircrews and mechanics for several aircraft squadrons based aboard the aircraft carriers USS *Langley*, USS *Saratoga*, and USS *Lexington*.

NAS Norfolk engaged in lighter-than-air (LTA) patrol operations from 1918 to 1924. These operations commenced with routine patrols flown by aircrews in kite balloons at NAS Hampton Roads in 1918 and supporting kite balloon flight operations from the kite balloon ship USS *Wright*, which was based at NOB Hampton Roads. NAS Norfolk also operated several patrol airships for patrol duty, most notably the Navy Airships C-3 and C-7. The C-7 was the first military airship to use helium as a lifting medium. The use of airships for patrol duty ceased at NAS Norfolk in 1924.

On September 27, 1922, NAS Norfolk achieved another naval aviation milestone when 18 Naval Aircraft Factory PT and Douglas DT-2 torpedo bombers from Torpedo and Bombing Plane Squadron One, based at NAS Norfolk, successfully performed the first mass torpedo practice attack against maneuvering ships. The aircraft carried out the mock attack against the battleship

USS *Arkansas*, registering eight hits on the dreadnought. This successful experiment served as a foreshadowing of naval warfare during World War II.

On November 5, 1923, NAS Norfolk conducted a series of fleet operational feasibility tests that successfully demonstrated the concept of stowing, assembling, and launching a seaplane from a surfaced submarine (the USS *S-1*) after it had been submerged. These tests were conducted using a Martin MS-1 as the test subject in the waters off Hampton Roads. The concept was once again proven on July 28, 1926, using the same submarine but a different aircraft, an XS-2 seaplane, off the coast of Norfolk. The concept of launching seaplanes from submarines was later utilized by the Japanese navy during World War II.

On November 13, 1926, the Schneider Trophy seaplane race was held at NAS Norfolk. The race was won by Maj. Mario de Barnardi, who piloted an Italian Macchi M.39, establishing world seaplane records of 248 mph over 100 and 200km. A Curtiss R3C-2 piloted by 1st Lt. Christian Frank Schilt, USMC, placed second. Successful World War II inline-engine fighter aircraft such as the USAAF Curtiss P-40 Tomahawk, USAAF North American P-51 Mustang, British Supermarine Spitfire, and Italian Macchi c.202 Folgore ("Thunderbolt") evolved in later years from the Schneider Trophy seaplane races.

During the 1930s, NAS Norfolk became one of the primary naval air stations for fleet acceptance flight trials for prototype naval aircraft. These years were the golden age of naval aviation and saw the rapid growth of shipboard aviation. At NAS Norfolk, catapult and arresting gear system development and testing were top priorities. With new aircraft carriers such as the *Ranger*, *Yorktown*, *Wasp*, and *Hornet* entering service, NAS Norfolk fulfilled the need to train their aircraft squadron aircrews in navigation, gunnery, and bombing. By September 1, 1939, NAS Norfolk possessed 236 acres of land, which included two operational airstrips: Chambers Field and West Landing Field.

Soon after the outbreak of World War II, NAS Norfolk began to directly support combat operations by conducting aerial anti-submarine patrols. These patrols were routinely performed by such NAS Norfolk–based patrol squadrons as VP-51, VP-52, VP-53, and VP-54.

Following the Japanese surprise attack on Pearl Harbor and America's entry into the war, NAS Norfolk formed new scouting and patrol squadrons to counter the threat posed to Allied shipping by Germany's stepped-up U-boat operations. Fleet Air Wing 5 was now organized under the command of the 5th Naval District and was comprised of 12 Vought OS2U Kingfisher seaplanes and PBY-5A Catalina flying boats belonging to VP-83 and VP-84. Throughout World War II, NAS Norfolk continued to train patrol squadron aircrews in ASW tactics.

Perhaps NAS Norfolk's most significant contribution to the Allied victory in World War II was its training of Allied naval aircrews. The majority of US naval air squadrons that participated in combat during the war trained at NAS Norfolk. This training was provided by Air Force Atlantic Fleet (AIRLANT), which produced both Atlantic and Pacific Fleet combat-ready carrier air units, patrol squadrons, and battleship and cruiser seaplane squadrons. From 1943 to 1945, AIRLANT trained approximately 326 US units.

During the post–World War II and post–Cold War eras, NAS Norfolk has served as the host for over 70 tenant commands. These have included numerous carrier groups, one carrier airborne early warning wing, one helicopter sea control wing, and various Naval Air Reserve units. One Marine Corps Reserve CH-46 Sea Knight helicopter squadron also called NAS Norfolk home. Some of the squadrons under these air wings participated in modern conflicts such as the Vietnam War, Operation Desert Storm, Operation Enduring Freedom, and Operation Iraqi Freedom. In 1968, NAS Norfolk was designated Recovery Control Center Atlantic, providing command, control, and communications support for recovery efforts of Apollo 7. NAS Norfolk has also helped to resolve national crises, such as in 1994 when 2,000 civilian workers, dependents, and non-essential military personnel at Guantanamo Bay Naval Base in Cuba needed to be airlifted to Norfolk as part of Operation Sincere Welcome.

During the 1990s, the Navy responded to the post–Cold War drawdown by initiating new directives at Navy shore installations aimed at cutting operating costs, enhancing efficiency, and making necessary adjustments required for a smaller Navy. In 1994, Naval Aviation Depot

Norfolk, which employed over 4,000 personnel involved in the repair of Grumman F-14 Tomcats and Grumman A-6 Intruders, closed. In 1999, NAS Norfolk was absorbed into Naval Station Norfolk, with its organizational core becoming the Air Department of Naval Station Norfolk and its airfield being named Naval Station Norfolk (Chambers Field). The Air Department of Naval Station Norfolk is now known as the Naval Station Norfolk Air Operations Department.

NAVAL STATION NORFOLK INSIGNIA. Naval Air Station Norfolk is now a part of Naval Station Norfolk, the world's largest naval base. (Courtesy of US Navy.)

One

IN THE BEGINNING 1915–1917

In 1915, American aviation pioneer Glenn H. Curtiss transferred his primary flight training and experimental aircraft construction operations from Buffalo, New York, to Newport News, Virginia, effectively establishing the Atlantic Coast Aeronautical Station in the process. The station's flight training operations were originally intended to train prospective civilian pilots, but in 1916 were extended to train prospective military pilots in the Army and Navy. Some of the first naval aviators to serve at NAS Hampton Roads (later NAS Norfolk) learned how to fly at the Atlantic Coast Aeronautical Station.

The prospective naval aviators who trained at the Atlantic Coast Aeronautical Station were known as the Naval Air Detachment, Curtiss Field, Newport News and began training on May 19, 1917. As stated by Amy Yarsinske in *Wings of Valor, Wings of Gold: An Illustrated History of U.S. Naval Aviation*, "As part of his comprehensive plan to eventually build a master naval facility at Norfolk, Secretary of the Navy Josephus Daniels added a proviso creating the Naval Reserve Flying Corps (NRFC), a group of student naval aviators, primarily from Harvard University, who had begun their training at the old Curtiss Field on May 19, 1917, and who would comprise the nucleus of seven students designated as Naval Air Detachment Hampton Roads." The Naval Air Detachment grew in size and scope of operations over the next five months, now including five officers, three aviators, ten enlisted sailors, and seven seaplanes.

THE ATLANTIC COAST AERONAUTICAL STATION. In this photograph, Atlantic Coast Aeronautical Station personnel pose for a group photograph in 1917. In the background is a lineup of aircraft based at the station: from left to right are (facing front) Curtiss JN twin-motor landplane (the first aircraft to be manufactured on the peninsula of Hampton Roads, Curtiss F-boat, Curtiss JN twin-motor seaplane, and Curtiss JN-4H Jenny; (facing hangars) Curtiss F-boat and Curtiss JN-4H Jenny. (Courtesy of Martin Copp via NASA Langley Research Center.)

Training Prospective NAS Hampton Roads Naval Aviators. Pictured is a Navy Curtiss R-6 seaplane on the seaplane ramp at the Atlantic Coast Aeronautical Station (Curtiss Flying School) in 1917. The woman in the dark shorts and top standing in the water near the port pontoon of the aircraft is Neta Snook, one of America's first aviatrixes, who, as the first woman trainee at the Atlantic Coast Aeronautical Station, helped to flight train many of NAS Hampton Roads' first naval aviators. Snook later served as Amelia Earhart's flight instructor. This aircraft was used to train prospective naval aviators on flying Navy seaplanes and is being shown off to another young woman. The Curtiss R-6 later briefly served as a torpedo bomber for the Navy. (Courtesy of Martin Copp.)

Major Air Power Proponent. Pictured in this group photograph of student pilots at the Atlantic Coast Aeronautical Station (Curtiss Flying School) is soon-to-be major airpower proponent William "Billy" Mitchell (center) of the Army, who learned to fly here. (Courtesy of Martin Copp.)

One of Naval Aviation's Founding Fathers. Glenn Curtiss (right), founder of the Atlantic Coast Aeronautical Station and one of naval aviation's founding fathers, and test pilot/instructor Victor Carlstrom inspect an experimental triplane at the station. (Courtesy of Martin Copp.)

Two

The Formative Years 1917–1920

In October 1917, the Naval Air Detachment moved its seaplane operations from the Curtiss Flying School in Newport News to Norfolk. Canvas hangars were set up near the shore to protect the aircraft. These operations served as the basis of an experimental seaplane base at Norfolk.

The missions of the new experimental seaplane base were to perform ASW patrols against German U-boats, conduct aviator and mechanic training, and perform fleet operational feasibility flight testing of aircraft and kite balloons. The Naval Air Detachment at Norfolk eventually gained recognition as a leading provider of trained naval aviators. On August 27, 1918, the detachment was designated NAS Hampton Roads, with Lt. Comdr. Patrick N.L. Bellinger commanding.

In 1918, a series of flight tests were conducted at NAS Hampton Roads involving flight operation of the Davis gun ASW weapon. It was found that the Curtiss HS-2 flying boat presented the best aerial platform for the Davis gun. However, World War I ended before it could be used in combat.

Also in 1918, experiments were conducted at NAS Hampton Roads involving the feasibility of flight operations from a sea sled, a small, high-speed motorboat. On November 15, 1918, high-speed trials involving the launching of an Italian Caproni Ca. 5 were conducted in the waters off Hampton Roads. It is unknown if the test was successful.

On March 7, 1919, a Navy Curtiss N-9 landplane flown by Lt. (jg) F.M. Johnson was successfully launched from a sea sled in the waters off NAS Hampton Roads. While this test proved the aircraft-carrying sea sled concept, it was not used in combat due to the end of World War I.

By the end of World War I, NAS Hampton Roads had grown to 167 officers, 1,227 enlisted men, and 65 aircraft.

Birthplace of a Naval Air Station. On September 8, 1917, an air training station / experimental seaplane base was established at Naval Operating Base, Hampton Roads, Virginia. This station became the first legitimate seaplane base in the United States. Pictured in this 1917 photograph are the first tent hangars set up at the Naval Air Detachment. Visible in the water are a Curtiss Model L-2 triplane (fourth from left) and Curtiss N-9 trainers. (Courtesy of Naval History and Heritage Command via Martin Copp via NASA Langley Research Center.)

First Tents and Seaplane Ramps at NAS Hampton Roads/Norfolk. Pictured are the first tents and seaplane ramps at the Naval Air Detachment, Naval Operating Base, Hampton Roads, in 1917. (Courtesy of Naval History and Heritage Command.)

Aeromarine Seaplane. Pictured is an Aeromarine seaplane at Hampton Roads in 1917. Note the early seaplane hangar in the background to the right. (Courtesy of Hampton Roads Naval Museum via NASA Langley Research Center.)

Tailless Swept-Wing Seaplane. Pictured is a Navy Burgess-Dunne seaplane at the Naval Air Detachment, Naval Operating Base, Hampton Roads in 1917. Two years earlier, on August 3, 1915, a naval aviator piloting a similar aircraft successfully spotted mortar fire from shore positions at Ft. Monroe in Hampton, Virginia. This military aviation milestone marked the first successful observance of ground fire from an aircraft in America. (Courtesy of Hampton Roads Naval Museum via NASA Langley Research Center.)

Balloon/Dirigible Hangar. Pictured is the balloon/dirigible hangar at NAS Hampton Roads in 1918. Inside the hangar, a blimp undergoes inflation. (Courtesy of Naval History and Heritage Command via Martin Copp.)

NAS Hampton Roads Officers' Quarters. Pictured are the officers' quarters at NAS Hampton Roads in 1918. (Courtesy of Naval History and Heritage Command via Martin Copp.)

NAS Hampton Roads Officers Row. Pictured is Officers Row at NAS Hampton Roads in 1918. (Courtesy of Naval History and Heritage Command via Martin Copp.)

NAS Hampton Roads Seaplane Basin Entranceway Arch. Pictured is the seaplane basin entranceway arch at NAS Hampton Roads in 1918. The arch was given as a gift by the government of Japan to the Jamestown Ter-Centennial Exposition on April 26, 1907. It served as an ornate fixture at NAS Hampton Roads/Norfolk for several years until it was torn down following the Japanese attack on Pearl Harbor in 1941. Note the aircraft hangars on the pier. (Courtesy of Naval History and Heritage Command via Martin Copp.)

East and West Piers at NAS Hampton Roads. Pictured are the East and West Piers at NAS Hampton Roads in 1918. Note the seaplane basin entranceway arch. (Both, courtesy of Naval History and Heritage Command via Martin Copp.)

EXPERIMENTAL CURTISS L-2 TRIPLANE SEAPLANE. An experimental Curtiss L-2 triplane seaplane is afloat in the seaplane basin at NAS Hampton Roads in 1918. (Courtesy of Naval History and Heritage Command via Martin Copp.)

AERIAL VIEW OF NAS HAMPTON ROADS. This aerial view shows the balloon/dirigible hangar and several administrative buildings in 1918. (Courtesy of Naval History and Heritage Command via Martin Copp.)

Boarding a Kite Balloon. Naval aviators board a tethered kite balloon at NAS Hampton Roads in 1918. Kite balloons were used by the Navy for scouting and observation duty. (Courtesy of Library of Congress via NASA Langley Research Center.)

Kite Balloon in Flight. Naval aviators perform a tethered flight in a kite balloon at Hampton Roads in 1918. (Courtesy of the Library of Congress via NASA Langley Research Center.)

Curtiss H-12 Flying Boat. A Curtiss H-12 flying boat takes off from NAS Hampton Roads on a wartime ASW patrol in 1918. (Courtesy of Hampton Roads Naval Museum via NASA Langley Research Center.)

Sopwith Schneider Seaplane. Pictured is a British-built Sopwith Schneider seaplane at NAS Hampton Roads in 1918. The paucity of American-made military aircraft made it imperative that the Army and Navy procure military aircraft from Allied nations. (Courtesy of Hampton Roads Naval Museum via NASA Langley Research Center.)

World War I Flying Boat. Pictured is a Curtiss H-16 flying boat on a trolley in front of a seaplane hangar at NAS Hampton Roads in 1918. Flight suitability experiments were conducted that year with an H-16, in which the forward observer on the aircraft operated a Davis gun, a recoilless rifle designed to be used against German U-boats. These experiments, in which a Curtiss HS-2 and Naval Aircraft Factory N-1 were also tested, showed that the Curtiss HS-2 was best suited for Davis gun operations. (Courtesy of NARA via NASA Langley Research Center.)

Davis Gun–Equipped Naval Aircraft Factory N-1 Seaplane. A naval aviator mans the Davis gun on a Naval Aircraft Factory N-1 "Sub Killer" Seaplane. The N-1 was specifically designed for ASW operations. (Courtesy of Naval History and Heritage Command.)

Naval Aircraft Factory N-1 "Sub Killer" Seaplane. Pictured is an N-1 "Sub Killer" seaplane used in Davis gun testing at NAS Hampton Roads in 1918. (Courtesy of NARA via NASA Langley Research Center.)

Davis Gun–Equipped Curtiss HS-2 Flying Boat. The forward observer operates a Davis gun aboard a Curtiss HS-2 flying boat in 1918. Flight testing at Hampton Roads in 1918 showed that this aircraft was best suited for the ASW weapon. (Courtesy of NARA.)

Early Wireless Radio–Equipped Flying Boat. Pictured is a radio-equipped Curtiss H-16 flying boat at NAS Hampton Roads on June 8, 1918. Note the antenna mounted on top of the rear fuselage of the aircraft. (Courtesy of NARA.)

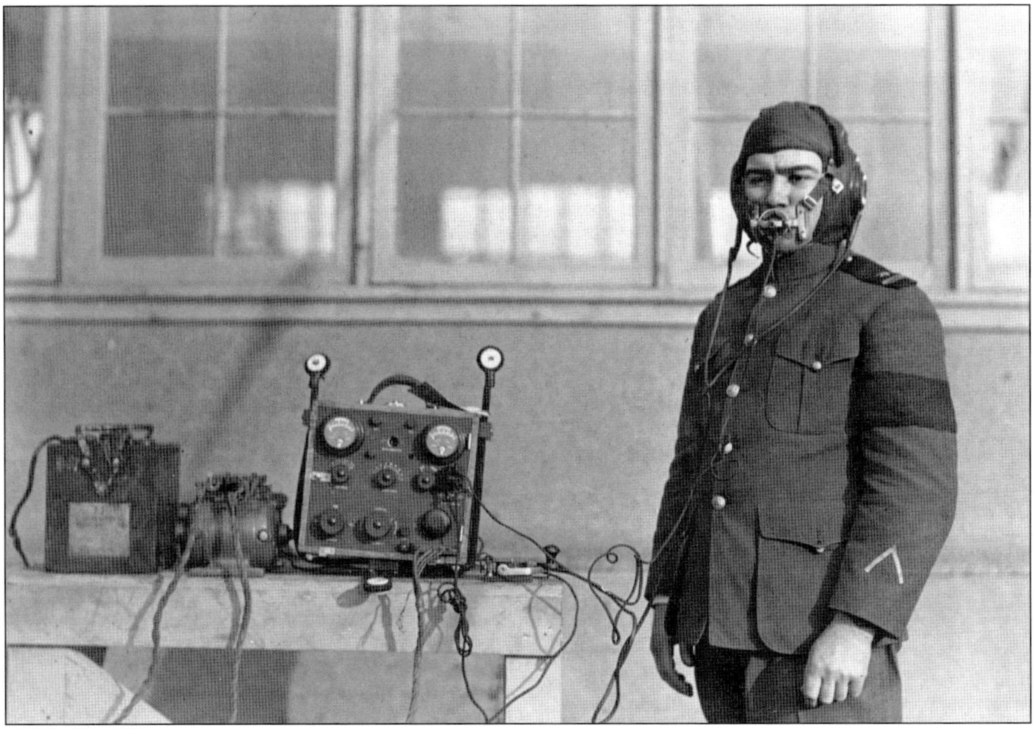

Early Aircraft Radio Telephone System. A naval aviator shows off an early aircraft radiotelephone system with headgear at NAS Hampton Roads. (Courtesy of NARA.)

Curtiss R-6 Seaplane on the Ramp. Pictured is a Curtiss R-6 seaplane on the ramp at NAS Hampton Roads on August 17, 1918. The Curtiss R-6 was also used by the Navy as an early torpedo bomber. (Courtesy of Naval History and Heritage Command.)

First of the Famous Curtiss NC Flying Boats. The first of the Curtiss NC flying boats, the NC-1, is tended to by sailors on the ramp at NAS Hampton Roads on November 9, 1918. The aircraft set a world record when it successfully performed a flight with 51 people aboard on November 25, 1918. It had to be written off, however, in May 1919, when it attempted to perform the first transatlantic flight and suffered irreparable damage. (Courtesy of Naval History and Heritage Command.)

Army Caproni Ca.5 Bomber/Sea Sled Flight Experiment. An Italian-built Caproni Ca.5 is prepared for high-speed trials on the deck of a sea sled at NAS Hampton Roads on November 14, 1918. (Courtesy of NARA via NASA Langley Research Center.)

Flight Experiment Preparation. A large group of sailors assist in the prepping of the Army's Caproni Ca.5 bomber aboard the sea sled on November 15, 1918. (Courtesy of the National Museum of Naval Aviation via NASA Langley Research Center.)

Awaiting High Speed Trials. The Caproni Ca.5 bomber, aboard a sea sled, awaits high-speed trials at Hampton Roads on November 15, 1918. (Courtesy of NARA via NASA Langley Research Center.)

Conducting Flight Experiment Preparations at Sea. Naval crews prepare for the sea sled experiment in the waters off NAS Hampton Roads on November 15, 1918. (Courtesy of the National Museum of Naval Aviation via NASA Langley Research Center.)

Sea Sled/Caproni Ca.5 Underway. Here are two views of the sea sled underway at Hampton Roads on November 15, 1918. Whether the aircraft was successfully launched from the sled or not is unknown. The sled was capable of reaching a speed of 65 mph without the bomber on board. (Above, courtesy of the National Museum of Naval Aviation via NASA Langley Research Center; below, courtesy of NARA via NASA Langley Research Center.)

CURTISS F-BOAT FLYING BOAT. A Curtiss F-boat flying boat taxies on the water at NAS Hampton Roads on November 24, 1918. (Courtesy of Naval History and Heritage Command.)

CURTISS N-9 TRAINER ABOARD A SEA SLED. A Curtiss N-9 trainer awaits flight experimentation at NAS Hampton Roads in February 1919. (Courtesy of NARA via NASA Langley Research Center.)

CURTISS N-9 TRAINER ON A SEA SLED. A Navy Curtiss N-9 landplane (with the engine running) undergoes preliminary suitability evaluations on a sea sled at NAS Hampton Roads on February 26, 1919. (Courtesy of NARA via NASA Langley Research Center.)

SEA SLED/CURTISS N-9 TRAINER UNDERWAY. A sea sled carrying a Curtiss N-9 Trainer ready for flight experimentation passes Fort Wool on March 7, 1919. Confederate general Robert E. Lee was stationed at Fort Wool prior to the Civil War while serving as an officer in the US Army. (Courtesy of the National Museum of Naval Aviation via NASA Langley Research Center.)

Lifting Off from a Sea Sled. A Navy Curtiss N-9 landplane piloted by Lt. (jg) F.M. Johnson lifts off from a sea sled following a successful launch on March 7, 1919. The sea sled was making a speed of 50 knots in the waters off NAS Hampton Roads at the time. The feat proved the viability of the aircraft-carrying sea sled concept and marked a significant milestone in the development of US naval aviation. (Both, courtesy of Martin Copp via NASA Langley Research Center.)

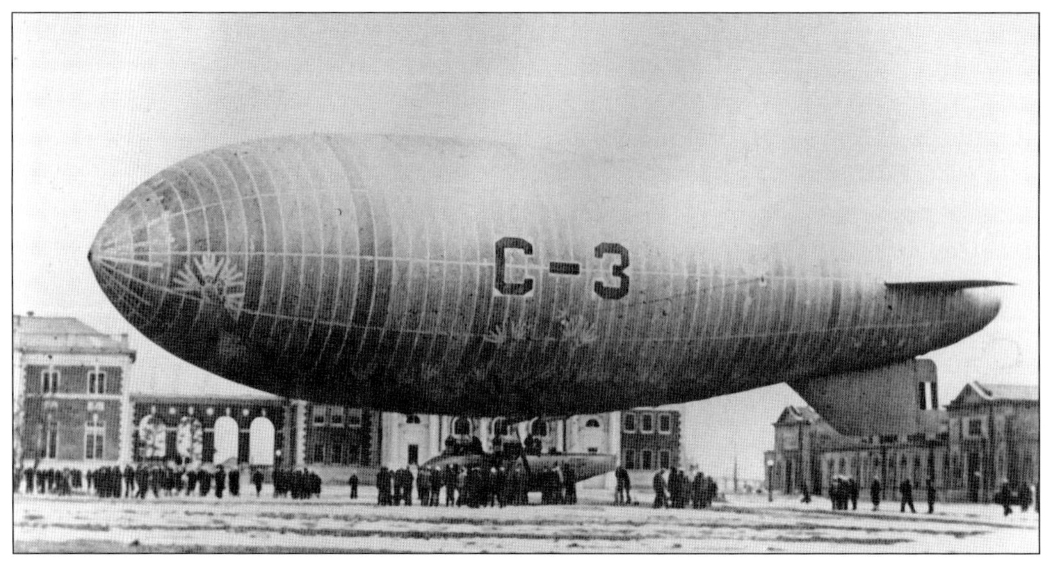

The Navy C-3 Dirigible. The US Navy C-3 dirigible patrol blimp is pictured at NAS Hampton Roads on June 11, 1920. The blimp, which used hydrogen as a lifting medium, caught on fire while performing a flight and burned at NAS Hampton Roads on July 7, 1921. (Courtesy of Hampton Roads Naval Museum via NASA Langley Research Center.)

Closeup of C-3 Dirigible. This closeup view of the C-3 patrol blimp at NAS Hampton Roads on June 11, 1920, shows the recovery parachute system on the envelope (lower side) of the blimp. (Courtesy of NARA.)

Three

SUPPORTING DEVELOPMENT OF THE USS *LANGLEY* 1921–1925

In August 1921, NAS Norfolk began to support the development of and flight operations aboard America's first aircraft carrier, the USS *Langley* (CV-1). That month, NAS Norfolk conducted a series of experimental tests that resulted in the development of arresting gear for the *Langley*. A dummy deck built on a turntable that could be turned into the wind was employed for the tests.

On August 11, 1921, NAS Norfolk pioneered carrier arresting gear when Lt. A.M. Pride taxied his Aeromarine aircraft onto the dummy deck and snared the arresting wires with the hook on his aircraft. On October 26, 1922, an Aeromarine 39-B piloted by Lt. Commander G. De Chevalier successfully performed the first landing on the *Langley*.

NAS Norfolk also developed a catapult system for the carrier. On November 18, 1922, Comdr. Kenneth Whiting, piloting a Naval Aircraft Factory PT torpedo bomber, successfully performed the first catapult launch from the *Langley* while the ship was anchored in the York River.

Norfolk played host to the *Langley's* air squadrons following the aircraft carrier's commissioning in 1922, training her aircrews and mechanics for several years. In the following years, the naval air station trained the aircrews and mechanics for several aircraft squadrons based aboard the aircraft carriers USS *Langley*, USS *Saratoga*, and *USS Lexington*.

Arresting Gear Turntable at NAS Norfolk. Pictured is the turntable that was used at NAS Norfolk for perfecting the arresting gear system that was to be outfitted on the rear flight deck of the USS *Langley*, America's first aircraft carrier. Aircraft could either perform taxiing or landings to simulate arrested landings on the aircraft carrier. (Courtesy of Martin Copp.)

The Pioneering of Carrier Arresting Gear. Lt. A.M. Pride taxies his Aeromarine 39-B onto the dummy deck at NAS Norfolk and snares the arresting wires with the hook on his aircraft on August 11, 1921. (Courtesy of Martin Copp via NASA Langley Research Center.)

Successful Arrested Landing Demonstration. An Aeromarine 39-B piloted by Lt. A.M. Pride successfully performs an arrested landing on the dummy deck turntable in September 1921. Note the hydrovane, a strut-like structure just forward of the landing gear. Hydrovanes were used on Navy aircraft to keep them from flipping over when making water landings. (Courtesy of NARA via NASA Langley Research Center.)

Rear View of Aeromarine Ensnared on Arresting Wires. Pictured is a rear view of the Aeromarine 39-B ensnared on the arresting wires on the dummy deck turntable. (Courtesy of the National Museum of Naval Aviation via NASA Langley Research Center.)

De Havilland DH-4 Ensnared on Arresting Wires. Pictured is a British-built de Havilland DH-4 ensnared on the arresting wires on the dummy deck turntable at NAS Norfolk. (Courtesy of the National Museum of Naval Aviation via NASA Langley Research Center.)

USS *Langley* at the Norfolk Naval Shipyard. Pictured is America's first aircraft carrier, the USS *Langley*, in port at the Norfolk Naval Shipyard in Portsmouth, Virginia, in 1922. Note the Aeromarine 39-B parked on the front section of the flight deck. (Courtesy of the Mariners Museum via NASA Langley Research Center.)

Aeromarine 39-B on the *Langley*. An Aeromarine 39-B is parked on the rear section of the *Langley's* flight deck in 1922. (Courtesy of NARA via NASA Langley Research Center.)

First Takeoff from an American Aircraft Carrier. A Vought VE-7 performs the first takeoff from the USS *Langley* in the waters off Cape Henry in Virginia Beach, Virginia, on October 17, 1922. Although detached to the *Langley*, the aircraft was home-based at NAS Norfolk. The VE-7 served as the Navy's first fighter aircraft and was also used as a trainer. Note the hydrovane on the front of the aircraft. (Courtesy of Martin Copp.)

Practicing Simulated Arrested Landings on the *Langley*. Lt. Comdr. G. De Chevalier, piloting an Aeromarine 39-B, practices on October 19, 1922, to perform the first arrested landing on the *Langley*. (Courtesy of Martin Copp via NASA Langley Research Center.)

Awaiting First Catapult Launch from *Langley*. Pictured is a Naval Aircraft Factory PT seaplane being prepped for the first catapult launch from the nation's first aircraft carrier, at anchor in the York River. This feat was accomplished on November 18, 1922, by Comdr. Kenneth Whiting, who piloted the aircraft. (Courtesy of NARA via NASA Langley Research Center.)

PT-2 Torpedo Bomber Detached to *Langley*. Pictured is a Naval Aircraft Factory PT-2 torpedo bomber detached to the *Langley* at Norfolk in 1922. Note the winged covered wagon squadron insignia, signifying that the aircraft was detached to America's first aircraft carrier. (Courtesy of NARA via NASA Langley Research Center.)

VOUGHT VE-7 LANDING ON THE *LANGLEY*. Pictured is a Vought VE-7 coming in for a landing on the flight deck of the *Langley* in 1922. The aircraft was home-based at NAS Norfolk. (Courtesy of NARA via NASA Langley Research Center.)

CURTISS TS-1 DETACHED TO *LANGLEY*. Pictured is a Curtiss TS-1 early biplane fighter detached to the *Langley* at NAS Norfolk in December 1922. (Courtesy of Martin Copp.)

Lineup of *Langley* Detached Aircraft. Pictured is a lineup of aircraft detached to the *Langley* on the tarmac at NAS Norfolk in April 1923. Aircraft visible include two Aeromarine 39-Bs, two Curtiss TS-1s, a British-built DeHavilland DH-4, and an airship in the air at far right. (Courtesy of NARA via NASA Langley Research Center.)

DT-2 Torpedo Bomber on Catapult Launch Mechanism. Pictured is a Douglas DT-2 landplane torpedo bomber on the catapult launch mechanism aboard the *Langley*. (Courtesy of Martin Copp via NASA Langley Research Center.)

DT-2 Seaplane Torpedo Bomber Awaiting Launch. A Douglas DT-2 seaplane torpedo bomber prepares for a catapult launch from the *Langley* in 1924. (Both, courtesy of Martin Copp via NASA Langley Research Center.)

DT-2 Torpedo Bomber in Flight. Pictured is a Douglas DT-2 landplane torpedo bomber, detached to the *Langley* and carrying a torpedo, in flight in 1925. Note the hydrovane. (Courtesy of Martin Copp via NASA Langley Research Center.)

Langley in the Waters of Hampton Roads. Pictured is the *Langley* at anchor in the waters of Hampton Roads during the mid-1920s. The carrier has a full complement of Vought VE-7s on the flight deck that were home-based at NAS Norfolk. (Courtesy of the Mariners Museum via NASA Langley Research Center.)

HOISTING A T2D-1 ABOARD THE *LANGLEY*. Pictured is a Douglas T2D-1, assigned to torpedo bomber squadron VT-2, being hoisted aboard the *Langley* at NOB Norfolk in 1927. The aircraft was being prepared to perform aircraft carrier suitability trials, which it performed successfully. The T2D-1 was the Navy's first twin-engine torpedo bomber to operate from an aircraft carrier. (Courtesy of NARA via NASA Langley Research Center.)

CURTISS F6C-2 HAWK BIPLANE FIGHTER. A Curtiss F6C-2 Hawk biplane fighter prepares for flight operations from the *Langley's* flight deck during the late 1920s. (Courtesy of Martin Copp.)

MARTIN T4M TORPEDO BOMBER LANDING. Above, a Martin T4M makes a landing approach to the *Langley* during the late 1920s. The T4M served as the Navy's primary carrier-borne torpedo bomber well into the 1930s. Below, the T4M has been successfully recovered aboard the *Langley*. (Both, courtesy of NARA via NASA Langley Research Center.)

MARTIN T4M FOLLOWING SUCCESSFUL ARRESTED LANDING. Pictured is a Martin T4M following a successful arrested landing aboard the *Langley* during the late 1920s. (Courtesy of NARA via NASA Langley Research Center.)

LANGLEY IN HAMPTON ROADS. Pictured is the *Langley* in the waters of Hampton Roads during the mid-to-late 1920s. Loening amphibian aircraft are visible on the flight deck. (Courtesy of the Mariners Museum via NASA Langley Research Center.)

Four

Burgeoning of Naval Aviation 1921–1929

On July 12, 1921, NAS Hampton Roads was re-designated NAS Norfolk, with Capt. S.H.R. Doyle commanding. In late July, NAS Norfolk played an important role supporting the battleship bombing experiments conducted off the Virginia coast that smashed the myth of "invincibility" of the World War I–vintage dreadnoughts. Aircraft based at Norfolk sank some of the ex-German World War I warships and registered bomb hits on the remote-controlled USS *Iowa*.

During the early 1920s, NAS Norfolk supported kite balloon flight operations from the USS *Wright*, which was based at NOB Hampton Roads. NAS Norfolk also operated several airships for patrol duty, most notably Airships C-3 and C-7. The C-7 was the first military airship to use helium as a lifting medium. In 1924, NAS Norfolk stopped using airships for patrol duty.

On September 27, 1922, eighteen Naval Aircraft Factory PT and Douglas DT-2 torpedo bombers from Torpedo and Bombing Plane Squadron One, based at NAS Norfolk, successfully performed the first mass torpedo practice attack against a maneuvering ship. The aircraft scored eight hits on the USS *Arkansas*.

On November 5, 1923, NAS Norfolk conducted a series of tests that successfully demonstrated launching a seaplane from a surfaced submarine (the USS *S-1*) after it had been submerged. These tests were conducted using a Martin MS-1 aircraft. The concept was once again proven on July 28, 1926, using the same submarine but an XS-2 seaplane, off the coast of Norfolk.

On November 13, 1926, NAS Norfolk hosted the Schneider Trophy seaplane race, won by Maj. Mario de Barnardi in an Italian Macchi M.39, establishing world closed-course seaplane records. A Curtiss R3C-2 piloted by 1st Lt. Christian Frank Schilt placed second in the race.

Early Parachute for Naval Aviators. At left, a naval aviator models a Jahn parachute, an early parachute for naval aviators, at NAS Hampton Roads on March 14, 1921. Below, the Jahn parachute is flight tested following bailout from a naval aircraft in the skies above Hampton Roads. (Both, courtesy of NARA via NASA Langley Research Center.)

WORLD WAR I–ERA FLYING BOATS. Pictured are two World War I Curtiss flying boats—an HS-2 (center) and H-12 (left)—parked in front of two seaplane hangars at NAS Hampton Roads in 1921. (Courtesy of Naval History and Heritage Command.)

NAVY MARTIN BOMBER IN FLIGHT. Pictured is a Navy Martin Bomber in flight above NAS Norfolk in late July 1921. This aircraft most likely took part in the battleship bombing experiments conducted off the Virginia coast that month. (Courtesy of the National Museum of Naval Aviation via NASA Langley Research Center.)

Navy Martin Bomber Landing at NAS Norfolk. Pictured is a Navy Martin Bomber landing at NAS Norfolk in late July 1921. Note the LTA hangar at left. This aircraft most likely took part in the vintage battleship bombing experiments. (Courtesy of the National Museum of Naval Aviation via NASA Langley Research Center.)

Direct Hit on a World War I German Submarine. A NAS Norfolk–based Curtiss F-5L flying boat scores a direct bomb hit, using a new lightweight bomb, on the ex–World War I German submarine U-117 during the vintage battleship bombing experiments. (Courtesy of Martin Copp.)

Remote-Controlled Bombing Target. Pictured is the USS *Iowa* under remote control from personnel aboard the USS *Ohio* (BB-12) during the battleship bombing experiments off the Virginia coast in July 1921. No personnel were aboard the *Iowa*, which sustained some hits from bombs dropped by Navy aircraft operating from NAS Norfolk. (Courtesy of Naval History and Heritage Command via Martin Copp.)

Gallaudet A-59 (D-4) Observation Seaplane. Pictured is a Gallaudet A-59 (D-4) observation seaplane at NAS Norfolk in 1921. (Courtesy of Hampton Roads Naval Museum via NASA Langley Research Center.)

Curtiss NC-7 Flying Boat. Pictured in the foreground is the Curtiss NC-7 flying boat, the seventh of ten in the famous NC series of large flying boats built by Curtiss, on the seaplane ramp at NAS Norfolk in 1921. In the background at left is a Gallaudet A-59 (D-4) observation seaplane. The Curtiss NC-4 flying boat was the first aircraft to successfully complete a transatlantic flight, in May 1919. (Courtesy of Naval History and Heritage Command via Martin Copp.)

Curtiss NC-9 Flying Boat. Pictured is the Curtiss NC-9 flying boat, the ninth of ten NC series large flying boats built by Curtiss, on the seaplane ramp at NAS Norfolk in 1921. (Courtesy of Naval History and Heritage Command via Martin Copp.)

LIBERTY TRACTOR MOTOR. Pictured is the center Liberty tractor motor on the Curtiss NC-8 flying boat, the eighth in the NC series of large flying boats built by Curtiss, in a seaplane hangar at NAS Norfolk on October 4, 1921. The Liberty series aircraft engines were powerful, reliable, and highly efficient. (Courtesy of NARA via NASA Langley Research Center.)

O-1 SEMI-RIGID AIRSHIP. Pictured is the Italian-built O-1 semi-rigid airship in flight above NAS Norfolk in 1921. The airship was used by the US Navy at NAS Norfolk to launch gliders that served as targets for anti-aircraft weapons. (Courtesy of Hampton Roads Naval Museum via NASA Langley Research Center.)

F-1 Blimp. Pictured is the Goodyear-built F-1 blimp at NAS Norfolk in 1921. The F-1 utilized both tractor and pusher motors and served as an engine testbed. (Courtesy of Martin Copp.)

Aircraft Engine Testbed Blimp. Pictured is an aircraft engine testbed blimp being towed back down to the ground via tether line by a group of sailors after successfully completing a test flight at NAS Norfolk in early 1922. (Courtesy of Hampton Roads Naval Museum via NASA Langley Research Center.)

KITE BALLOON TENDER. Pictured is the kite balloon tender USS *Wright* (AZ-1) in port at NOB Norfolk (now Naval Station Norfolk) in July 1922. NAS Norfolk supported kite balloon flight operations from the *Wright*. The ship was named in honor of Orville Wright, one of the Wright brothers. On July 16, 1922, the final tethered flight of a kite balloon from the *Wright* was made, after which the kite balloon was permanently assigned to NAS Norfolk. (Courtesy of NARA via NASA Langley Research Center.)

USS *WRIGHT* KITE BALLOON TENDER. Pictured is an artist's rendering by Rose Stokes of a kite balloon making a tethered flight from the *Wright* at sea. (Courtesy of Naval History and Heritage Command via NASA Langley Research Center.)

Aircraft Engine Testbed Blimp in Flight. Pictured is an aircraft engine testbed blimp in flight above NAS Norfolk in 1922. Note the flotation gear on the landing skids of the aircraft fuselage control car beneath the dirigible. (Courtesy of Martin Copp.)

Aerial Torpedo Practice. The battleship USS *Arkansas* is pictured with an unarmed torpedo about to hit, launched from one of 18 PT and DT-2 torpedo bombers from Torpedo and Bombing Plane Squadron One based at NAS Norfolk, with a Naval Aircraft Factory PN-9 flying boat flying over in the observation role off the Virginia Capes (Cape Charles and Cape Henry) on September 27, 1922. This exercise was part of the effective demonstration of the first mass aerial torpedo practice attack against maneuvering ships and served as a foreshadowing of combat in World War II. (Courtesy of US Navy.)

DT-2 Practice Aerial Torpedo Strike. The first unarmed torpedo hit is scored on the battleship *Arkansas* by a Torpedo and Bombing Plane Squadron One Douglas DT-2, piloted by Lieutenant Grey, on September 27, 1922. (Courtesy of US Navy.)

US Navy C-7 Airship. The C-7 Airship performs a flight above NAS Norfolk in October 1922. This airship was the first to use helium as a lifting medium. It was retired from service later in 1922. (Courtesy of NARA via NASA Langley Research Center.)

Fokker FT-1 Torpedo Bomber. A Navy Dutch-built Fokker FT-1 torpedo bomber is in flight above NAS Norfolk in April 1923. (Courtesy of NARA via Naval History and Heritage Command.)

New Aircraft Hangars. Pictured are new aircraft hangars on the new land extension at NAS Norfolk in May 1923. A Navy twin-engine Martin Bomber and DH-4 single-engine observation aircraft are in the foreground. To the right of the Martin bomber is a lineup of Vought VE-7s. (Courtesy of Martin Copp via NASA Langley Research Center.)

Loening M-3 Kitten. Pictured is a Loening M-3 Kitten floatplane at NAS Norfolk. The Kitten was specially designed for use aboard battleships and submarines. (Courtesy of NARA via NASA Langley Research Center.)

Martin MS-1 Scout. The Martin MS-1 Scout seaplane used in submarine operational feasibility studies at NOB Norfolk is at NAS Norfolk in 1923. (Courtesy of NARA via NASA Langley Research Center.)

MS-1 Stowage Tank. Pictured is the MS-1 stowage tank aboard the submarine USS *S-1* at NOB Norfolk in October 1923. Below, the tank has been opened, revealing a disassembled, stowed MS-1 Scout seaplane. (Both, courtesy of NARA via NASA Langley Research Center.)

Taking MS-1 Out of its Stowage Tank. The crew of the *S-1* takes the MS-1 out of its stowage tank aboard the submarine at NOB Norfolk. (Courtesy of Hampton Roads Naval Museum via NASA Langley Research Center.)

Conducting MS-1/Submarine Operational Feasibility Testing. Crews are testing the feasibility of stowing and launching a Martin MS-1 Scout seaplane from the *S-1* submarine at NOB Norfolk on November 5, 1923. (Courtesy of Martin Copp via NASA Langley Research Center.)

MS-1 Recovery aboard the USS *S-1*. The MS-1 has been successfully recovered aboard the *S-1* following launch from the submarine at NOB Norfolk. (Courtesy of Hampton Roads Naval Museum via NASA Langley Research Center.)

Visit by Rear Admiral Moffett. Pictured is a visit to NAS Norfolk by Rear Adm. William A. Moffett (center) and Captain Yarnell (right) in March 1924. Moffett received the Medal of Honor earlier in his military career, served as the initial leader of the US Navy Bureau of Aeronautics, and is widely recognized as the architect of US naval aviation. (Courtesy of NARA.)

Torpedo and Bombing Squadron One DT-2S. Pictured are Douglas DT-2s of Torpedo and Bombing Squadron One at NAS Norfolk in 1925. (Courtesy of Martin Copp via NASA Langley Research Center.)

Beached Fokker FT-1 Torpedo Bomber. A beached Fokker FT-1 torpedo bomber is parked in front of a hangar at NAS Norfolk on June 12, 1925. (Courtesy of NARA via Naval History and Heritage Command.)

Seaplane/Submarine Operational Feasibility Testing at Sea. On July 28, 1926, the Navy successfully demonstrated the feasibility of deploying and recovering a Cox-Klemin XS-2 seaplane from the *S-1* off the coast of Norfolk. (Courtesy of NARA via NASA Langley Research Center.)

Schneider Trophy Seaplane Racer. A Curtiss R3C-4 seaplane racer, piloted by Lt. George T. Cuddihy, is prepped for launching at the seaplane basin at NAS Norfolk during the Schneider Trophy seaplane race on November 13, 1926. Cuddihy did not place among the top four winners of the race. (Courtesy of NARA via NASA Langley Research Center.)

SCHNEIDER TROPHY WINNER, 1926. Italian major Mario de Bernardi climbs out of the cockpit of his Macchi M.39 racer at NAS Norfolk after completing a trial flight on November 10, 1926, prior to the 1926 Schneider Trophy Seaplane Race held on November 13 at NAS Norfolk. (Courtesy of NARA.)

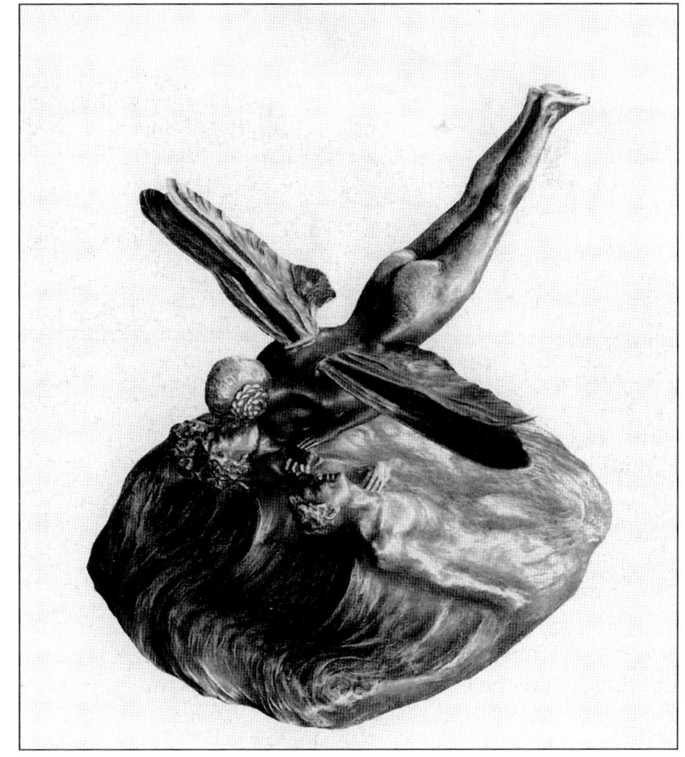

JACQUES SCHNEIDER TROPHY. Pictured is the Jacques Schneider Trophy, which was awarded to Maj. Mario de Bernardi for piloting his Macchi M.39 racer to victory in the 1926 Schneider Trophy Seaplane Race. (Courtesy of NARA.)

Beaching a PN-10 Flying Boat. A team of sailors prepare to beach a Naval Aircraft Factory PN-10 flying boat at NAS Norfolk on November 24, 1926. (Courtesy of NARA via NASA Langley Research Center.)

Martin T3M-2 Torpedo Bomber. Pictured is a Martin T3M-2 torpedo bomber at NAS Norfolk in 1927. T3M-2s were assigned to both land bases and aircraft carriers. (Courtesy of NARA via NASA Langley Research Center.)

Towing an F-5L from a Warship. During the late 1920s, feasibility testing was conducted at NAS Norfolk in which a Curtiss F-5L flying boat was successfully towed behind a Navy warship. (Courtesy of NARA via NASA Langley Research Center.)

Loening XHL-1 in Flight. Pictured is a Loening XHL-1 amphibious staff transport in flight above NAS Norfolk in 1928. (Courtesy of Martin Copp.)

Airship/Aircraft Parasite Feasibility Flight Testing. Seen here is a Martin T-4M in flight above NAS Norfolk during the late 1920s trailing a hook to hook onto an airship in flight during an airship/aircraft parasite feasibility flight test experiment. The test was a success and gave the Navy confidence to request the development of large airships capable of serving as aerial aircraft carriers. (Courtesy of NARA via NASA Langley Research Center.)

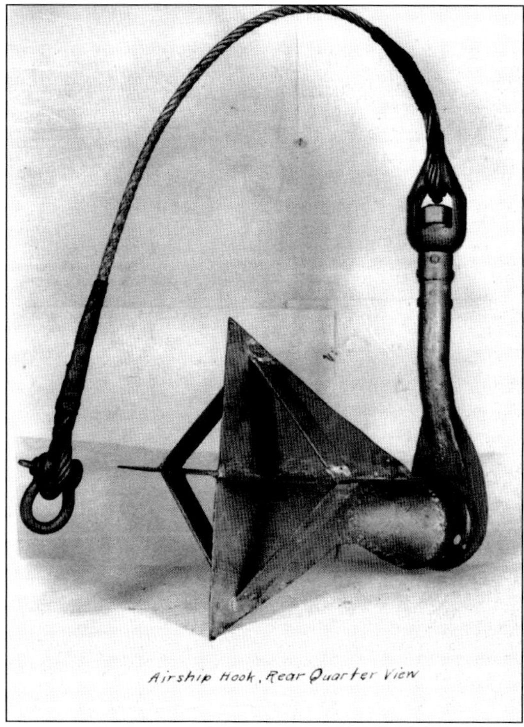

Aerial Airship Hook. This is an aerial airship hook used in the airship/aircraft parasite feasibility flight testing experiments conducted in the skies above Norfolk in the late 1920s. (Courtesy of NARA via NASA Langley Research Center.)

Dornier DO-X "Aerial Oceanliner." The German Dornier DO-X is moored in the waters off NAS Norfolk in 1929 above. The DO-X represented the manifestation of the aerial oceanliner concept pursued by numerous aircraft companies throughout the world at the time. The aircraft was making a goodwill visit to America. Below, the DO-X is making a takeoff from the waters around Norfolk. (Both, courtesy of NARA.)

Dornier DO-X in Flight. Pictured is the German Dornier DO-X in flight above NAS Norfolk in 1929. The massive size of the aircraft dazzled spectators in the Hampton Roads area during its successful visit. (Courtesy of NARA.)

Five

THE GOLDEN YEARS OF NAVAL AVIATION 1930–1941

The 1930s saw NAS Norfolk become one of the primary naval air stations for performing fleet acceptance flight trials for prototype naval aircraft. NAS Anacostia in Washington, DC, also established as an experimental seaplane base in 1917, similarly performed flight trials for prototype naval aircraft and assumed this role until the establishment of NAS Patuxent River in southern Maryland, which took over the majority of this role in 1943.

The 1930s marked the golden age of naval aviation, which saw a rapid expansion of shipboard aviation. At NAS Norfolk, catapult and arresting gear systems were further developed and enhanced through experimental flight testing, including the development of aircraft landing barrier systems aboard aircraft carriers. New aircraft carriers, such as the *Ranger*, *Yorktown*, *Wasp*, and *Hornet*, were now entering service, and NAS Norfolk fulfilled the need to train their aircraft squadron aircrews in navigation, gunnery, bombing, and aerial torpedo practice.

Also during the 1930s, flying boats were being produced by American aircraft manufacturers with significantly enhanced range capabilities. As a result, some of these aircraft established new world distance records for nonstop flights, flying from NAS Norfolk to destinations in Latin America.

By September 1, 1939, NAS Norfolk spanned 236 acres of land, which included two operational airstrips: Chambers Field and West Landing Field.

Seaplane Trainers. Pictured is a lineup of Consolidated NY-1 seaplane trainers at NAS Norfolk in 1931. Note the arch at the seaplane basin entrance at upper left. (Courtesy of NARA via NASA Langley Research Center.)

Seaplane Trainer in Flight. A Consolidated NY-1 seaplane trainer is in flight above the waters near NAS Norfolk in 1931. (Courtesy of NARA via NASA Langley Research Center.)

The Navy's First Dive Bomber. Pictured is the Curtiss XF8C-7 Helldiver, the prototype of the Navy's first dive-bomber, parked on the tarmac at NAS Norfolk in 1931. The aircraft was undergoing fleet acceptance flight trials. Its design featured two fixed machine guns in the upper wing, and fixed landing gear. (Courtesy of NARA.)

Vought O2U Corsair Tractorized Landing Gear Testbed. Pictured is a Vought O2U Corsair testbed used in aircraft tractorized landing gear feasibility testing at NAS Norfolk in 1931. (Courtesy of NARA via NASA Langley Research Center.)

Loening XO2L-1 Amphibian. The Loening XO2L-1 Amphibian prototype was the only aircraft of its series designation to see service with the Navy. It is seen here preparing for a test flight at NAS Norfolk in June 1931. This aircraft was to perform the amphibious observation role for the Navy. (Both, courtesy of NARA via NASA Langley Research Center.)

Loening XO2L-1 Rough-Water Sea Trials. The Loening XO2L-1 is performing rough-water sea trials at NAS Norfolk. (Courtesy of NARA via NASA Langley Research Center.)

Naval Aircraft Factory XP4N-1 Flying Boat. The Naval Aircraft Factory XP4N-1 flying boat, prototype of the P4N-1 flying boat series, is preparing to perform fleet acceptance trials at NAS Norfolk in 1931. (Courtesy of NARA via NASA Langley Research Center.)

Hall-Aluminum XP2H-1 Flying Boat. The Hall-Aluminum XP2H-1 taxies on the water during rough water sea trials at NAS Norfolk in 1932. The aircraft, designed as an experimental long-range patrol flying boat, was the largest four-engine biplane to serve the Navy. The only one of its type, it was flown in 1935 on a nonstop flight from NAS Norfolk to Coco Solo, Panama Canal Zone. The flight lasted over 25 hours. (NARA via NASA Langley Research Center.)

Curtiss F6C-3 Hawk Fighter. Pictured is a Curtiss F6C-3 Hawk in flight above NAS Norfolk in 1932. Hawks were used by the Navy as both aircraft carrier–based and land-based fighters during the late 1920s and early 1930s. (NARA via NASA Langley Research Center.)

FIRST MODERNIZED NAVAL FIGHTER FLIGHT TRIALS. The Grumman XFF-1, prototype of the first US naval fighter to feature an enclosed cockpit and canopy as well as retractable landing gear, undergoes fleet acceptance flight trials in the skies above Norfolk in 1932. (Both, courtesy of NARA via NASA Langley Research Center.)

Martin PM-2 Flying Boat Sea Trials. A Martin PM-2 flying boat is undergoing smooth water sea trials at NAS Norfolk in 1932. The aircraft is performing a smooth-water takeoff. (Courtesy of NARA via NASA Langley Research Center.)

First of the Consolidated Flying Boat Series. Pictured is a Consolidated P2Y-1 flying boat, the first of Consolidated's great flying boat series that included the famous PBY Catalina, in flight above NAS Norfolk in 1933. On September 7–8, 1933, a formation of six Consolidated P2Y-1s commanded by Lt. Comdr. H.E. Holland set a formation flight distance record flying nonstop from Norfolk to Panama. (Courtesy of NARA via NASA Langley Research Center.)

CONSOLIDATED P2Y-1 FLYING BOAT IN FLIGHT. Here is another view of a Consolidated P2Y-1 flying boat above NAS Norfolk in 1933. (Courtesy of NARA via NASA Langley Research Center.)

GRUMMAN XF2F-1 FIGHTER IN FLIGHT. The Grumman XF2F-1, a prototype of the F2F-1 fighter series, is undergoing flight and fleet acceptance trials above NAS Norfolk in late 1933. (Courtesy of NARA via NASA Langley Research Center.)

Grumman XSF-2 Scout Aircraft in Flight. A Grumman XSF-2 scout is undergoing flight and fleet acceptance trials at NAS Norfolk in 1934. (Courtesy of NARA via NASA Langley Research Center.)

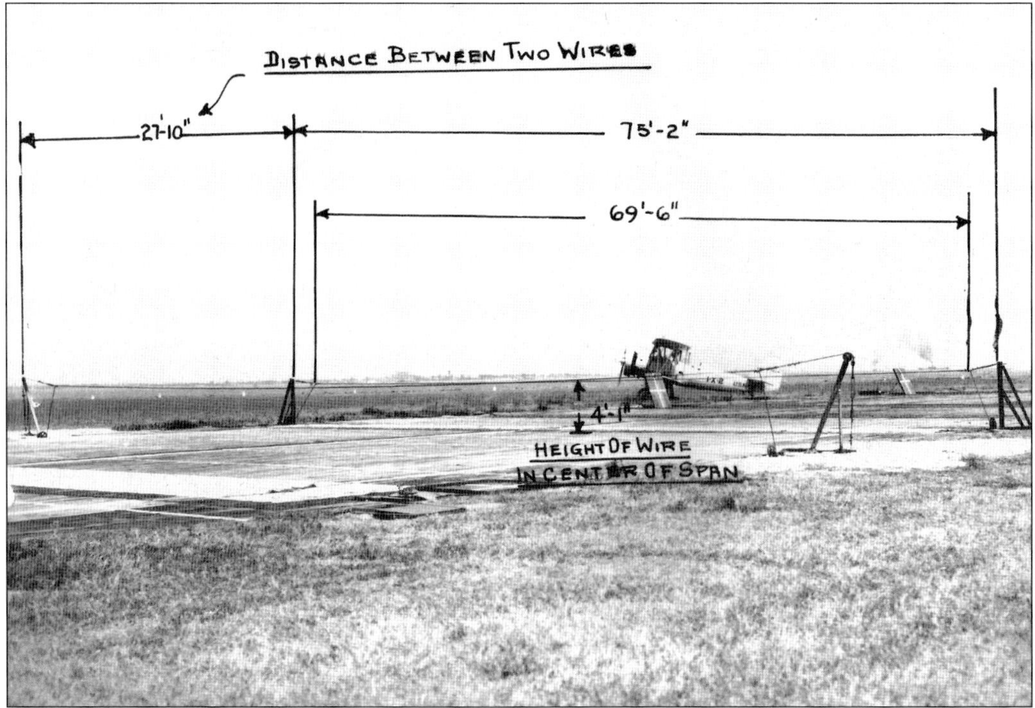

Aircraft Carrier Landing Barrier Test Setup. Pictured is an aircraft carrier landing barrier test setup arrangement at NAS Norfolk in 1934. The naval air station was heavily involved in testing some of the first carrier landing barrier systems. (Courtesy of NARA via NASA Langley Research Center.)

Successful Aircraft Carrier Landing Barrier Engagement. A Vought O3U Corsair observation aircraft successfully engages a landing barrier during a test at NAS Norfolk on June 14, 1934. (Courtesy of NARA via NASA Langley Research Center.)

Failed Landing Barrier Engagement. Pictured is the Martin XT5M-1, which failed to successfully engage a test landing barrier at NAS Norfolk in June 1934. (Courtesy of NARA via NASA Langley Research Center.)

Measuring Arresting Tail Rise. The arresting tail rise moments are being measured on this Grumman SF-1 scout aircraft at NAS Norfolk in 1934. (Courtesy of NARA via NASA Langley Research Center.)

Grumman JF-1 Duck Amphibian. Pictured is a Grumman JF-1 Duck amphibian at NAS Norfolk in September 1934. The Duck was used by the Navy as an air-sea rescue asset during the first few years of American participation in World War II. (Courtesy of NARA via NASA Langley Research Center.)

Curtiss BF2C-1 Goshawk Fighter. Pictured is a Curtiss BF2C-1 Goshawk fighter at NAS Norfolk in October 1934. The Goshawk was the last Curtiss fighter to see service with the Navy, serving for only a short time due to numerous problems with its landing gear. (Courtesy of NARA via NASA Langley Research Center.)

Great Lakes BG-1 Carrier-Based Dive Bomber. Pictured is a Great Lakes BG-1 carrier-based dive bomber belonging to VB-3B (assigned to either the USS *Ranger* or USS *Lexington*) at NAS Norfolk in February 1935. (Courtesy of NARA via NASA Langley Research Center.)

Hook Down, Gear Down, Canopy Open. The Grumman XF3F-2 fighter, prototype of the F3F fighter series, performs fleet acceptance flight trials over NAS Norfolk in June 1935. The F3F was the immediate predecessor to the more famous F4F Wildcat. (Courtesy of NARA via NASA Langley Research Center.)

Northrop XBT-1 Monoplane Dive Bomber. The Northrop XBT-1 monoplane dive bomber, an early developmental prototype of the famous Douglas SBD dive bomber, is performing flight trials for the Navy above NAS Norfolk in 1935. (Courtesy of NARA via NASA Langley Research Center.)

Great Lakes XB2G-1 Dive Bomber. Pictured is the Great Lakes XB2G-1 dive bomber, featuring retractable landing gear, performing flight trials for the Navy above NAS Norfolk in 1936. (Courtesy of NARA via NASA Langley Research Center.)

Brewster XSBA-1 Monoplane Scout Bomber. Pictured is the Brewster XSBA-1 monoplane scout bomber performing flight trials for the Navy above Hampton Roads in 1936. (Courtesy of NARA via NASA Langley Research Center.)

Sikorsky XPBS-1 Patrol Flying Boat. The huge Sikorsky XPBS-1 patrol flying boat is taking off from the waters near NAS Norfolk in 1937. The aircraft was performing flight trials for the Navy at the time. (Courtesy of NARA.)

Grumman F3F-1 Fighter. Pictured is a Grumman F3F-1 fighter at NAS Norfolk in April 1940. The F3F-1 was the predecessor of the famous F4F Wildcat fleet defender. (Courtesy of NARA.)

Vindicator on Floats. The Vought XSB2U-3 Vindicator seaplane prototype undergoes rough water sea trials at NAS Norfolk in 1941. The Vindicator dive bomber served with both the Navy and US Marine Corps well into World War II. (Courtesy of NARA via NASA Langley Research Center.)

Douglas TBD-1 Devastator Torpedo Bombers. Pictured is a lineup of Torpedo Squadron Five (VT-5) Douglas TBD-1 Devastator torpedo bombers at NAS Norfolk in September 1941. Note the lineup of Douglas SBD Dauntless dive bombers to the left. (Courtesy of Naval History and Heritage Command.)

Six

Helping Turn the Tide of World War II 1941–1945

Following the start of World War II, NAS Norfolk commenced aerial anti-submarine patrols. These patrols were flown by such NAS Norfolk–based squadrons as VP-51, VP-52, VP-53, and VP-54.

Once America officially entered the war, NAS Norfolk formed new scouting and patrol squadrons to counter the increasing German U-boat threat. Fleet Air Wing 5 was now organized under the command of the 5th Naval District and was comprised of 12 Vought OS2U Kingfisher seaplanes and PBY-5A Catalina flying boats belonging to VP-83 and VP-84. For the duration of the war, NAS Norfolk trained patrol squadron aircrews in ASW tactics.

NAS Norfolk's most significant contribution to the Allied victory in World War II, however, was its training of Allied naval aircrews. The majority of US naval air squadrons that participated in combat during the war trained at Norfolk. Naval aircrews performed fighter tactical training flights, bombing practice flights, and torpedo practice flights in their aircraft. This training was provided by AIRLANT, which produced both Atlantic and Pacific Fleet "combat-ready" carrier air units, patrol squadrons, and battleship and cruiser seaplane squadrons. From 1943 to 1945, AIRLANT trained approximately 326 US naval air units. All of the US naval aircrews that participated in the Battles of the Coral Sea, Midway, and Santa Cruz trained for combat at NAS Norfolk.

On October 12, 1942, the Naval Air Center, commanded by Capt. J.M. Shoemaker, was established at NAS Norfolk to serve as the command center for operations at Norfolk. Fields close to Norfolk were utilized in training, patrol plane, practice bombing, and aerial gunnery operations. The assembly and repair department workforce grew from 213 enlisted men and 573 civilians in 1939 to 3,561 civilians and 4,852 military personnel at the end of the war. These workers, including many women, performed engine and fuselage overhauls.

Devastator Torpedo Bomber Combat Preparation. Pictured is a Torpedo Squadron Five (VT-5) Douglas TBD-1 Devastator torpedo bomber undergoing combat preparation by a maintenance crew at NAS Norfolk in December 1941. (Courtesy of Naval History and Heritage Command.)

Martin PBM Mariner Flying Boat Lineup. Pictured is a lineup of Martin PBM Mariner flying boats at NAS Norfolk in 1942. The Mariner was one of the types of flying boats used by the Navy for anti-submarine patrols off the East Coast. The aircraft was responsible for sinking several German U-boats during World War II. (Courtesy of NARA.)

Servicing an Aircraft Engine. Sailors service the engine of a Vought SB2U Vindicator dive bomber at NAS Norfolk in 1942. The Vindicator was the predecessor of the famous Douglas SBD Dauntless dive bomber. (Courtesy of NARA.)

The Landing Field, Early 1942. This view of Chambers Field at NAS Norfolk on February 10, 1942, includes two lineups of Grumman F4F Wildcats in the foreground. (Courtesy of NARA.)

TBDs with Folded Wings. Several Douglas TBD-1 Devastator torpedo bombers are pictured with folded wings at NAS Norfolk on February 10, 1942. (Courtesy of NARA.)

Taxiing Wildcat. A Grumman F4F Wildcat is taxiing down the landing field at NAS Norfolk on February 10, 1942. (Courtesy of NARA.)

Wildcats on the Landing Field. Pictured are a pair of Grumman F4F Wildcats parked on the landing field in front of a hangar at NAS Norfolk on February 10, 1942. (Courtesy of NARA.)

The Flight Line, Early 1942. This is a view of the flight line at NAS Norfolk on February 11, 1942. (Courtesy of NARA.)

Advance Base "A" Training Unit, Hangar No. 2. These interior views of Advance Base "A" Training Unit, Hangar No. 2 at Breezy Point, NAS Norfolk are from May 1942. This facility served as both working and sleeping quarters for 1,100 men. The aircraft are Consolidated PBY Catalina flying boats used for ASW tactical and patrol training missions. (Both, courtesy of NARA.)

VOUGHT OS2U KINGFISHER SEAPLANE ROLLOUT. A Vought OS2U Kingfisher seaplane is being rolled out of a hangar at NAS Norfolk in early May 1942. The Kingfisher was used by the Navy and Marine Corps as an ASW patrol aircraft during World War II. It carried a depth charge beneath each wing. (Courtesy of NARA via Naval History and Heritage Command.)

NAS NORFOLK FLIGHT LINE. This view of the flight line at NAS Norfolk is from July 1942. Aircraft visible include one Grumman TBF Avenger torpedo bomber, three Grumman F4F Wildcat fighters, and five Naval Aircraft Factory N3N trainers. (Courtesy of NARA.)

SBD, TBF, and F4F Aircraft. Pictured is an arrangement of SBDs, TBFs, and F4Fs parked in front of a hangar at NAS Norfolk in September 1942. (Courtesy of NARA.)

Varied Aircraft Arrangement. Various aircraft are parked in front of a hangar at NAS Norfolk in September 1942. Aircraft visible include a TBF and SBD in the foreground and a pair of British Fleet Air Arm Tarpons (US–supplied TBFs) parked in front of the hangar in the background. (Courtesy of NARA.)

SBD Training Mission Embarkment. This Douglas SBD Dauntless dive bomber (affectionately dubbed "Slow But Deadly" by its aircrews) is embarking on a training mission at NAS Norfolk in September 1942. In early June of that year, SBDs from the US aircraft carriers *Yorktown*, *Hornet*, and *Enterprise* smashed the Japanese navy's fleet of four carriers at the Battle of Midway, helping to turn the tide of the war in the Pacific. (Courtesy of NARA.)

SBD in Flight. An SBD based at NAS Norfolk is performing a training flight above the Atlantic Ocean in September 1942. (Courtesy of NARA.)

Corsair in Flight. A Chance Vought F4U Corsair is in flight above Norfolk in September 1942. The Corsair was one of the Navy's premier fleet defenders at the time. Together with the Grumman F6F Hellcat, the Navy's other premier fighter at the time, the Corsair helped the Navy achieve air superiority in the Pacific during World War II. Note the "birdcage" canopy hood on the aircraft, signifying that this was an early variant of the Corsair series. (Courtesy of NARA.)

NAS Norfolk–Based VF-17 Corsairs in Flight. This formation of NAS Norfolk–based Fighter Squadron 17 (VF-17) "Jolly Rogers" Chance Vought F4U-1A Corsairs are in flight above Bougainville in early March 1944. Aircraft No. 29 is piloted by Lt. (jg) Ira Kepford, the Navy's top-scoring ace (16 "kills") at the time. VF-17 was one of the Navy's most successful fighter squadrons of the war in the Pacific. (Courtesy of NARA via Naval History and Heritage Command.)

Martin PBM-3 Mariner Flying Boat in Flight. A Martin PBM-3 Mariner flying boat is performing an ASW patrol mission above Hampton Roads in September 1942. The aircraft featured a powerful radar system housed in a giant radome atop the forward section of the fuselage, just aft of the cockpit/canopy. (Courtesy of NARA via Naval History and Heritage Command.)

Avenger Torpedo Attack Practice. NAS Norfolk–based Grumman TBF-1 Avenger torpedo bombers practice torpedo attacks in November 1942. The nearest TBF has just dropped a Mk. XIII torpedo equipped with a plywood tail shroud. (Courtesy of NARA via Naval History and Heritage Command.)

Avengers in Flight. A formation of Grumman TBF-1 Avenger torpedo bombers are in flight near NAS Norfolk in November 1942. The Avenger proved to be an invaluable ASW aerial asset for the Allies, sinking numerous German U-boats during World War II. (Courtesy of NARA.)

Wildcat in Flight. Pictured is a Grumman F4F Wildcat wearing an Atlantic Theater paint scheme in flight over NAS Norfolk in December 1943. (Courtesy of NARA.)

NAVY LIBERATORS IN FLIGHT. NAS Norfolk–based Consolidated PB4Y-1 Liberators are pictured in December 1943. The aircraft above is on an ASW patrol mission over the Atlantic, and the one at right is in flight over Norfolk. NAS Norfolk–based Liberators, deployed to bases in England and South America, sank numerous German U-boats during World War II. (Both, courtesy of NARA.)

Helldiver Formation over Chesapeake Bay Entrance. A formation of NAS Norfolk–based Curtiss SB2C Helldiver dive bombers fly over the entrance to the Chesapeake Bay in December 1943. The land visible is Virginia's eastern shore. Helldivers caused considerable damage to Japanese shipping during the later years of the war. (Courtesy of NARA.)

Helldiver Formation Return Flight. A formation of NAS Norfolk–based Curtiss SB2C Helldiver dive bombers return to the Hampton Roads area after a training mission in December 1943. (Courtesy of NARA.)

New Hangar Construction. This aerial view shows new hangar construction at NAS Norfolk in August 1944. At left is a lineup of Martin PBM-3 Mariner flying boats and two Navy biplane trainers. (Courtesy of Martin Copp via NASA Langley Research Center.)

View of a Mariner from Another Mariner. Here is a view of a Martin PBM-3S Mariner flying boat as seen through the twin tails of another PBM-3S at NAS Norfolk on March 1, 1945. (Courtesy of NARA via Naval History and Heritage Command.)

NAS Norfolk Women Mechanics. A group of women mechanics proceed to their work area at NAS Norfolk in early 1945. This team included both Navy Women Accepted for Volunteer Emergency Service (WAVES) members and Women Marines. The WAVES consisted of women belonging to the US Naval Reserve who made service contributions to the American war effort during World War II. (Courtesy of NARA via Naval History and Heritage Command.)

From the Control Tower. This is an interior view of a control tower at NAS Norfolk in early 1945. Note the WAVES member at left. Also, note the Vought OS2U Kingfisher seaplanes on the seaplane ramp in the background. (Courtesy of NARA via Naval History and Heritage Command.)

Seven

Maintaining Supremacy during the Cold War 1946–1994

During the post–World War II and post–Cold War eras, NAS Norfolk hosted over 70 tenant commands. These commands have included numerous carrier groups, one carrier airborne early warning wing, one helicopter sea control wing, and various Naval Air Reserve units. One Marine Corps Reserve CH-46 Sea Knight helicopter squadron was also home-based at NAS Norfolk. Some of the squadrons under these air wings participated in the Vietnam War, Operation Desert Storm, Operation Enduring Freedom, and Operation Iraqi Freedom.

One of the Grumman E-2 Hawkeye early-warning aircraft squadrons, the VAW-124 "Bullseye Hummers," later known as the "Bear Aces," home-based at NAS Norfolk, saw combat during the Vietnam War beginning in 1970 aboard the aircraft carrier USS *America*. In 1977, the squadron received the COMNAVAIRLANT Battle Efficiency Award and the Command Retention Silver Anchor Award. In 1980, the squadron vectored several Navy and Air Force fighters for intercepts of Soviet Tupolev TU-95 "Bear" reconnaissance bombers, thus changing their squadron name to the "Bear Aces." On August 19, 1981, VAW-124 vectored two VF-41 Grumman F-14 Tomcats toward two Libyan Sukhoi SU-22 "Fitter" fighter aircraft, which were promptly shot down, during the Gulf of Sidra incident. The squadron once again saw combat on January 21, 1991, during Operation Desert Storm, vectoring CVW-8 strike aircraft toward Iraqi targets in Kuwait.

In 1968, NAS Norfolk was designated Recovery Control Center Atlantic, providing command, control, and communications support for recovery efforts of Apollo 7. NAS Norfolk has also helped to resolve national crises, such as in 1994 when 2,000 civilian workers, dependents, and nonessential military personnel at Guantanamo Bay needed to be airlifted to Norfolk as part of Operation Sincere Welcome.

MARTIN AM MAULER ASSEMBLY LINE. Pictured is an assembly line of Martin AM Mauler carrier-borne attack aircraft at NAS Norfolk on February 17, 1950. The Mauler was designed during World War II. (Courtesy of NARA.)

GRUMMAN F8F BEARCAT ASSEMBLY LINE. Grumman F8F Bearcat fighter aircraft are on the assembly line in Building V-60 at NAS Norfolk on February 27, 1950. The Bearcat was the Navy's premier piston-engine fleet defender at the time. (Courtesy of NARA.)

Douglas JD Assembly Line. Douglas JD attack bombers are on the assembly line in Building V-90 at NAS Norfolk on February 28, 1950. The JD was the Navy's version of the Air Force's Douglas A-26 Invader attack bomber. (Courtesy of NARA.)

Interior View of the Fuselage Shop. The Fuselage Shop in Building V-28 at NAS Norfolk is pictured on February 28, 1950. (Courtesy of NARA.)

Tigercat Pulse Jet Drone Carrier. A Grumman F7F-2U Tigercat carrying two pulse jet drones is in flight above Norfolk on August 9, 1950. (Courtesy of NARA.)

Firefighting Demonstration. This firefighting demonstration was put on by Naval Air Station Fire Department officials for students at NAS Norfolk in December 1950. An open tank fire is being put out with a foamite stream. (Courtesy of NARA.)

Grumman AF-2 Guardian Formation in Flight. A formation of Grumman AF-2W equipped with search radars, affectionately called "guppies," and AF-2S Guardian hunter ASW aircraft of VS-801 are in flight over NAS Norfolk in October 1952. (Courtesy of NARA.)

View of Breezy Point, 1960. In this 1960 aerial view of Breezy Point at NAS Norfolk, Martin P5M Marlin ASW flying boats are parked in front and to the side of the air traffic control tower/hangar. (Courtesy of US Navy.)

Sikorsky SH-3A Sea King Helicopters. A pair of Sikorsky SH-3A Sea King helicopters belonging to the NAS Norfolk home-based anti-submarine squadron Helicopter Squadron Five (HS-5) "Night Dippers," assigned to the aircraft carrier USS *Essex* (CVS-9), are in flight in 1967 above the North Atlantic. The helicopters were participating in joint exercises between the US and Dutch navies. (Courtesy of US Navy.)

Grumman E-1B Tracer. This Grumman E-1B Tracer belonging to the NAS Norfolk home-based Carrier Airborne Early Warning Squadron 121 (VAW-121) "Griffins," assigned to the aircraft carrier USS *Franklin D. Roosevelt* (CVA-42), is pictured in flight in 1971. (Courtesy of US Navy via National Museum of Naval Aviation.)

VAW-124 Grumman E-2B Hawkeye. A NAS Norfolk home-based Carrier Airborne Early Warning Squadron 124 (VAW-124) "Bullseye Hummers" Grumman E-2B Hawkeye lands on the aircraft carrier USS *America* (CVA-66) in the Mediterranean Sea in 1971. VAW-124, once again assigned to the *America*, deployed to Southeast Asia in late 1972 through early 1973 to support the US war effort in Vietnam. (Courtesy of US Navy.)

VAW-123 Grumman E-2B Hawkeye. Pictured is a NAS Norfolk home-based Carrier Airborne Early Warning Squadron 123 (VAW-123) "Screwtops" Grumman E-2B Hawkeye following landing on the aircraft carrier USS *Saratoga* (CVA-60) off the coast of Vietnam in 1972. (Courtesy of US Navy.)

Deep Submergence Rescue Vehicle Delivery. The deep-submergence rescue vehicle DSRV-2 is delivered to the Navy at NAS Norfolk on July 8, 1975. The DSRV-2 is being moved from an Air Force Military Airlift Command (MAC) C-141 Starlifter to a trailer for transport to NOB Norfolk. (Courtesy of NARA.)

Sea Knight Helicopter/Diver Practice Exercise. Pictured is a NAS Norfolk–based Helicopter Combat Squadron Six (HC-6) Boeing Vertol HU-46 Sea Knight helicopter winching in two Navy divers during a practice exercise on June 13, 1980. (Courtesy of NARA.)

VAW-126 E-2C Hawkeye Carrier Landing. A NAS Norfolk–based Carrier Airborne Early Warning Squadron 126 (VAW-126) E-2C Hawkeye performs a landing on the aircraft carrier USS *John F. Kennedy* (CV 67) during a NATO exercise on October 19, 1986. (Courtesy of NARA.)

Statue of Liberty Flyby. A NAS Norfolk–based Carrier Airborne Early Warning Squadron 126 (VAW-126) flys by the Statue of Liberty on November 1, 1986. (Courtesy of NARA.)

VAW-124 E-2C Hawkeyes. Two NAS Norfolk–based Carrier Airborne Early Warning Squadron 124 (VAW-124) E-2C Hawkeyes are in flight on November 10, 1986. (Courtesy of NARA.)

VAW-121 E-2C Hawkeye Awaiting Catapult Launch. A NAS Norfolk–based Carrier Airborne Early Warning Squadron 121 (VAW-121) E-2C Hawkeye awaits launch from the USS *Dwight D. Eisenhower* (CVN 69) No. 2 catapult on February 26, 1988. (Courtesy of NARA.)

VAW-121 E-2C HAWKEYE CATAPULT LAUNCH. The VAW-121 E-2C Hawkeye in the previous image is seen here being launched from the *Dwight D. Eisenhower's* No. 2 catapult. (Courtesy of NARA.)

VAW-120 E-2C HAWKEYE. A NAS Norfolk–based Carrier Airborne Early Warning Squadron 120 (VAW-120) "Greyhawks" Grumman E-2C Hawkeye performs a landing taxi-in at NAS Oceana, Virginia, on August 1, 1989. VAW-120 serves as an E-2 training squadron. (Courtesy of US Navy.)

VAW-120 C-2A Greyhound. A NAS Norfolk–based Carrier Airborne Early Warning Squadron 120 (VAW-120) "Greyhawks" Grumman C-2A Greyhound performs a landing taxi-in at NAS Oceana, Virginia, on August 1, 1989. (Courtesy of US Navy.)

HM-15 MH-53E Mine Countermeasures Exercise. A NAS Norfolk–based Helicopter Mine Countermeasures Squadron 15 (HM-15) Sikorsky MH-53E Sea Dragon helicopter tows a Mark 105 hydrofoil minesweeping sled during a simulated mine-clearing mission in a harbor on November 1, 1989. (Courtesy of US Navy.)

Minesweeping Under a Rainbow. A NAS Norfolk–based Helicopter Mine Countermeasures Squadron 15 (HM-15) Sikorsky MH-53E Sea Dragon helicopter performs a mine countermeasures sortie under a rainbow near NAS Alameda, California, on September 1, 1990. (Courtesy of US Navy.)

Operation Desert Storm VAW-123 E-2C Hawkeye. A NAS Norfolk–based Carrier Airborne Early Warning Squadron 123 (VAW-123) "Screwtops" Grumman E-2C Hawkeye is in flight during Operation Desert Storm in 1991. (Courtesy of US Navy.)

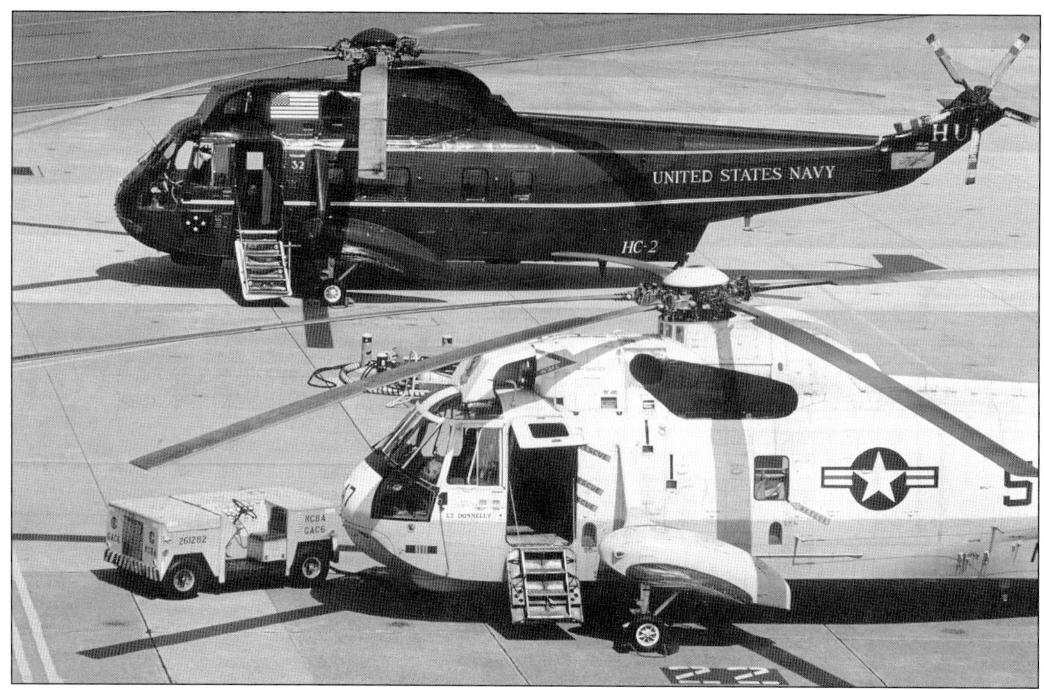

Pair of HC-2 Sea King Helicopters. Pictured are a pair of NAS Norfolk–based helicopter combat support Squadron Two (HC-2) Sikorsky VH-3A and SH-3G Sea King helicopters at NAS Oceana, Virginia, on March 27, 1991. (Courtesy of US Navy.)

President Clinton Visits. Air Force One is at rest on the tarmac at NAS Norfolk on October 6, 1994, during the arrival of Pres. Bill Clinton in Norfolk to express his gratitude to sailors and their families for supporting Operation Uphold Democracy off the coast of Haiti. (Courtesy of NARA.)

Eight

Helping the Navy Now and in the Future 1995–Present

The 1990s saw the US Navy initiate new directives at shore installations aimed at cutting operating costs, enhancing efficiency, and making necessary adjustments required for a smaller Navy. In 1994, Naval Aviation Depot Norfolk, which was responsible for the repair of Grumman F-14 Tomcats and Grumman A-6 Intruders, closed. In 1999, NAS Norfolk became part of Naval Station Norfolk, with its organizational core becoming the Air Department of Naval Station Norfolk and its airfield now being named Naval Station Norfolk (Chambers Field). The Air Department of Naval Station Norfolk is currently known as Naval Station Norfolk Air Operations Department.

Since 1995, numerous E-2 Hawkeye early warning/command and control aircraft squadrons and various helicopter squadrons home-based at NAS Norfolk have participated in combat. In 1999, Carrier Airborne Early Warning Squadron 124 (VAW-124) was deployed aboard the USS *Theodore Roosevelt* (CVN 71) and saw combat directing airstrikes on targets in Kosovo. The *Theodore Roosevelt* later deployed to the Persian Gulf, where VAW-124 helped US air assets enforce the no-fly zone in the skies above Iraq during Operation Southern Watch. Following the terrorist attacks of September 11, 2001, VAW-124, now aboard the USS *Enterprise* (CVN 65), helped direct airstrikes against the Taliban in Afghanistan during Operation Enduring Freedom. In 2003, VAW-124, based aboard the *Theodore Roosevelt*, participated in combat missions in support of Operation Iraqi Freedom.

Helicopter Mine Countermeasures Squadron 14 (HM-14), home-based at NAS Norfolk, provided airborne mine countermeasures (AMCM) support during Operation Iraqi Freedom in 2003. When the invasion of Iraq was launched in 2003, HM-14 participated in the de-mining of the waters surrounding the port of Umm Qasr. As a result, the port was reopened, and humanitarian relief efforts were able to reach beleaguered Iraqi civilians. HM-14 is currently deployed to several Eastern Pacific countries and continues to perform the AMCM mission.

The Naval Station Norfolk Air Operations Department currently hosts five carrier airborne early warning squadrons operating E-2 Hawkeyes, one fleet logistics support squadron operating C-2 Greyhounds, three helicopter mine countermeasures squadrons operating MH-53E Sea Dragons, and eight helicopter sea combat squadrons operating MH-60S Knighthawks.

NAS Norfolk Military Airlift Command (MAC) Terminal. In this aerial view of the NAS Norfolk MAC Terminal on June 25, 1995, an Air Mobility Command Lockheed C-5 Galaxy transport is parked on the tarmac. (Courtesy of NARA.)

NAS Norfolk Administration And Control Tower Building. Seen here is an aerial view of the NAS Norfolk Administration and Control Tower Building on June 25, 1995. (Courtesy of NARA.)

HS-5 Sikorsky SH-60F Seahawk Helicopter. A NAS Norfolk–based Helicopter Anti-Submarine Squadron Five (HS-5) "Nightdippers" Sikorsky SH-60F Seahawk performs a simulated ASW mission over the western Mediterranean on June 19, 1996, while the *Sturgeon*-class attack submarine USS *Grayling* (SSN-646) remains surfaced in the background. (Photograph by AF2 Jim Vidrine, courtesy of US Navy.)

VAW-126 E-2C Hawkeye Catapult Launch Prep. A Naval Station Norfolk–based Carrier Airborne Early Warning Squadron 126 (VAW-126) "Seahawks" Grumman E-2C Hawkeye is prepped for a catapult launch from the USS *Harry S. Truman* (CVN 75) on January 15, 2001. The carrier was operating in the Persian Gulf to support Operation Southern Watch. (Courtesy of NARA.)

VAW-123 E-2C Hawkeye Catapult Launch. A Naval Station Norfolk–based VAW-123 "Screwtops" Grumman E-2C Hawkeye is pictured just prior to catapult launch from the *Theodore Roosevelt* on March 16, 2001. (Courtesy of NARA.)

VRC-40 Northrop Grumman C-2A Greyhound. A Naval Station Norfolk–based Fleet Logistics Support Squadron 40 (VRC-40) "Rawhides" carrier onboard delivery (COD) Northrop Grumman C-2A Greyhound is at rest on the tarmac at Naval Station Norfolk on July 22, 2002. (Courtesy of NARA.)

Cargo Ramp Down. The C-2A Greyhound in the previous image is pictured here with cargo ramp down on the tarmac at Naval Station Norfolk on July 22, 2002. (Courtesy of NARA.)

Moving a VAW-124 E-2C Hawkeye. Flight deck crews aboard the *Theodore Roosevelt*, operating in the Mediterranean, guide a Naval Station Norfolk–based Carrier Airborne Early Warning Squadron 124 (VAW-124) "Bear Aces" Northrop Grumman E-2C Hawkeye around the carrier's flight deck on February 18, 2003. (Photograph by Photographer's Mate Airman Brad Garner, courtesy of US Navy.)

VAW-123 E-2C HAWKEYE CATAPULT LAUNCH. A Naval Station Norfolk–based Carrier Airborne Early Warning Squadron 123 (VAW-123) "Screwtops" E-2C Hawkeye lifts off the flight deck of the *Enterprise*, operating in the Atlantic, following catapult launch on September 2, 2003. (Photograph by Photographer's Mate Airman Jason W. Pfiester, courtesy of US Navy.)

MAIL AND CARGO DELIVERY AT SEA. A Naval Station Norfolk–based Helicopter Combat Support Squadron Six (HC-6) "Chargers" Sikorsky MH-60S Seahawk (Knighthawk) helicopter assigned to the USS *George Washington* (CVN 73) delivers mail and cargo to the fast combat support ship USNS *Supply* (T-AOE 6) on February 27, 2004. (Courtesy of NARA.)

Ammunition Delivery at Sea. This Naval Station Norfolk–based Helicopter Combat Support Squadron Six (HC-6) "Chargers" Sikorsky MH-60S Knighthawk is delivering ammunition from the *Tarawa*-class amphibious assault ship USS *Saipan* (LHA 2) to a nearby Navy warship on July 13, 2004. (Courtesy of NARA.)

VR-56 McDonnell Douglas C-9B Skytrain II in Flight. A Naval Station Norfolk–based Fleet Logistics Squadron 56 (VR-56) "Globemasters" McDonnell Douglas C-9B Skytrain II aircraft flies above Naval Station Norfolk on August 1, 2004. VR-56 is a logistics support provider serving all branches of the US armed forces. (Courtesy of NARA.)

VAW-123 E-2C Air Show Fly-By. A Naval Station Norfolk–based VAW-123 "Screwtops" E-2C Hawkeye performs an audience fly-by at the 2004 "In Pursuit of Liberty" Naval Air Station Oceana air show on September 25, 2004. (Photograph by AF2 Daniel J. McLain, courtesy of US Navy.)

HC-8 Vertical Replenishment (VERTREP) Mission. Pictured is a Naval Station Norfolk–based Helicopter Combat Support Squadron Eight (HC-8) "Dragon Whales" MH-60S Knighthawk performing a VERTREP mission between the *Sacramento*-class fast combat support ship USS *Seattle* (AOE 3, center) and the *Wasp*-class amphibious assault ship USS *Essex* (LHD 2, left) on September 29, 2004, in the northern Persian Gulf. (Courtesy of NARA.)

HC-8 Vertrep Mission. Seen here from the helicopter interior are aircrew members of a Naval Station Norfolk–based HC-8 "Dragon Whales" MH-60S Seahawk (Knighthawk) helicopter hooking up a cargo pallet aboard the USS *Seattle* during a VERTREP mission in the Persian Gulf on December 6, 2004. The aircraft carrier in the background is the *John F. Kennedy*. (Courtesy of NARA.)

VAW-126 E-2C Carrier Launch. A Naval Station Norfolk–based VAW-126 "Seahawks" E-2C is launched from the *Harry S. Truman* in the Persian Gulf on December 10, 2004. The aircraft was embarking on a close air support mission during Operation Iraqi Freedom. (Photograph by Photographer's Mate Airman Ryan O'Connor, courtesy of US Navy.)

VRC-40 C-2A Greyhound Movement aboard a Carrier. Boatswain's mate first class (AB1) Henry Cooper guides a Naval Station Norfolk–based VRC-40 "Rawhides" C-2A Greyhound around the flight deck of the *Theodore Roosevelt* on June 23, 2005. The *Roosevelt* was participating in a training exercise in the Atlantic at the time. (Courtesy of NARA.)

HSC-26 MH-60S Seahawk Cast and Recovery Training. A Naval Station Norfolk–based Helicopter Sea Combat Squadron 26 (HSC-26) Detachment 3 (DET 3) MH-60S Seahawk performs cast and recovery training with 2nd Fleet Antiterrorism Security Team Marines on June 25, 2005. (Courtesy of NARA.)

HSC-28 MH-60S Knighthawk SAR Mission. Crew members of a Naval Station Norfolk–based Helicopter Sea Combat Squadron 28 (HSC-28) MH-60S Knighthawk perform a search-and-rescue mission above a severely flooded New Orleans, Louisiana, during the aftermath of Hurricane Katrina on August 31, 2005. (Courtesy of NARA.)

HSC-28 Hurricane Katrina Humanitarian Assistance Support. An HSC-28 SH-60 Seahawk helicopter places a load of pallets aboard the *Wasp*-class amphibious assault ship USS *Bataan* (LHD 5) in the Gulf of Mexico to provide support for Hurricane Katrina humanitarian assistance operations on September 1, 2005. (Courtesy of NARA.)

HM-14 Hurricane Katrina Disaster Relief. Naval Station Norfolk–based Helicopter Mine Countermeasures Squadron 14 (HM-14) CH-53 Sea Stallion aircrew members unload supplies for Hurricane Katrina survivors in New Orleans on September 5, 2005. (Courtesy of NARA.)

Unloading Water For Hurricane Katrina Survivors. Pictured are Naval Station Norfolk–based HM-14 CH-53 Sea Stallion aircrews unloading water for Hurricane Katrina survivors in New Orleans on September 5, 2005. (Courtesy of NARA.)

Supplying MRE to Hurricane Rita Survivors. These HM-14 pilots unload meals, ready to eat (MRE), for Hurricane Rita survivors in Mississippi on September 24, 2005. (Courtesy of NARA.)

VAW-126 E-2C Hawkeye Carrier Arrested Landing. Pictured is a Naval Station Norfolk–based VAW-126 "Seahawks" E-2C Hawkeye performing an arrested landing aboard the *Harry S. Truman* during the aircraft carrier's qualifications and sustainment training with Carrier Air Wing Three (CVW-3) off the East Coast on October 13, 2005. (Courtesy of NARA.)

HSC-26 Seahawk Helicopter Takeoff Prep. A Naval Station Norfolk–based Helicopter Sea Combat Squadron 26 (HSC-26) MH-60S Seahawk prepares for takeoff at Naval Station Norfolk on April 27, 2006. Below, aviation warfare systems operator second class Matthew Hartman gives the "all clear" signal for takeoff. (Both, courtesy of NARA.)

VAW-124 Change of Command Ceremony. Comdr. Kenneth W. Caraveo (left) receives command of Carrier Airborne Early Warning Squadron 124 (VAW-124) from Comdr. Robert L. Mason during a change of command ceremony at Naval Station Norfolk on April 27, 2006. (Courtesy of NARA.)

VAW-124 E-2C Aircraft Dedication. This E-2C Hawkeye was dedicated to the new squadron commander Kenneth "Cheech" Caraveo during the change of command ceremony on April 27, 2006. (Courtesy of NARA.)

HSC-2 Seahawk Helicopter Formation Landing Practice. Two Naval Station Norfolk–based Helicopter Sea Combat Squadron Two (HSC-2) MH-60S Seahawk helicopters practice formation landings at Fort Pickett, Virginia, on January 24, 2007. (Photograph by MC1 Steven Harbour, courtesy of US Navy.)

Military Joint Training Exercise. A Naval Station Norfolk–based MH-53 Sea Dragon helicopter has just deployed soldiers from the 237th Military Police Company, New Hampshire Army National Guard during a joint training exercise at Fort Pickett, Virginia, on February 20, 2007. (Courtesy of US Army and Sgt. Matthew Kuzma via NARA.)

HM-14 MH-53 Helicopter Heavy Airlift Mission. A Naval Station Norfolk–based Helicopter Mine Countermeasures Squadron 14 (HM-14) "Vanguard" MH-53 Sea Dragon helicopter performs a heavy lift mission—airlifting a sling-loaded high-mobility multipurpose wheeled vehicle—during a joint training exercise at Fort Pickett, Virginia, on February 21, 2007. (Courtesy of US Army and Sgt. Jon Soucy via NARA.)

Coming in for an Arrested Recovery. Here, a Naval Station Norfolk–based VAW-126 "Seahawks" E-2C Hawkeye comes in for an arrested recovery on the *Harry S. Truman*, operating in the Atlantic on September 17, 2007. (Photograph by Sn. Kevin T. Murray Jr., courtesy of US Navy.)

VAW-124 E-2C Hawkeye on Middle East Mission. A Naval Station Norfolk–based VAW-124 "Bear Aces" E-2C Hawkeye is in flight above the Gulf of Oman on March 25, 2009. (Photograph by MC3 Jonathan Snyder, courtesy of US Navy.)

HM-15 Haiti Earthquake Relief Mission. Soldiers assist the aircrew of a Naval Station Norfolk–based HM-15 "Blackhawks" MH-53E Sea Dragon helicopter assigned to the aircraft carrier USS *Carl Vinson* (CVN 70) in delivering food and supplies to earthquake survivors at the airport in Port-au-Prince, Haiti, on January 15, 2010. (Photograph by MC1 Daniel Barker, courtesy of US Navy.)

HM-14 Haiti Earthquake Relief Mission. Pictured is a Naval Station Norfolk–based HM-14 "Vanguard" MH-53E Sea Dragon helicopter carrying vital supplies landing in Port-au-Prince to deliver its cargo to earthquake survivors on January 16, 2010. The helicopter was assigned to the *Carl Vinson*. (Photograph by MC1 Daniel Barker, courtesy of US Navy.)

HSC-9 MH-60S Seahawk Fleet Training Mission. A Naval Station Norfolk–based Helicopter Sea Combat Squadron Nine (HSC-9) "Eightballers" MH-60S Seahawk is in flight on a fleet training mission over the Atlantic on February 27, 2010. The helicopter was assigned to the aircraft carrier USS *George H.W. Bush* (CVN 77). (Photograph by MC3 Nicholas Hall, courtesy of US Navy.)

VRC-40 C-2A Greyhound Catapult Launch. This is a Naval Station Norfolk–based VRC-40 "Rawhides" Northrop Grumman C-2A Greyhound being catapult-launched from the *George H.W. Bush* in the Atlantic on June 11, 2010. The aircraft wears a paint scheme commemorating VRC-40's establishment 50 years before. (Photograph by MCSN Daniel S. Moore, courtesy of US Navy.)

VAW-120 E-2C Hawkeye Arrested Landing. A Naval Station Norfolk–based Carrier Airborne Early Warning Squadron 120 (VAW-120) "Greyhawks" E-2C Hawkeye makes an arrested landing aboard the *George H.W. Bush*, performing a training mission in the Atlantic on September 22, 2010. (Photograph by MCSN Kevin J. Steinberg, courtesy of US Navy.)

Facilitating a Carrier Visit by the Admiral. This image captures the arrival of Adm. Bill Gortney, commander of US Fleet Forces Command, via a Naval Station Norfolk–based Helicopter Sea Combat Squadron Nine (HSC-9) "Tridents" HH-60H Seahawk for a visit aboard the *Dwight D. Eisenhower* in the Atlantic on July 3, 2013. (Courtesy of defenseimagery.mil and Mass Communication Specialist Seaman Andrew Schneider.)

HM-14 Formation Flight Training. An HM-14 MH-53E Sea Dragon performs formation flight training over Naval Station Norfolk on April 20, 2016. The occasion marked the first time since 2006 that the helicopter squadron performed a flight with five aircraft. (Photograph by MC1 David Kolmel, courtesy of US Navy.)

Joyful Homecoming. Naval aircrewman mechanical second class Gary Penrod of VRC-40 reunites with his family during a homecoming celebration at Naval Station Norfolk on July 11, 2016. VRC-40 returned home following an eight-month deployment aboard the *Harry S. Truman*. (Photograph by MC3 Kayla King, courtesy of US Navy.)

HM-14 MH-53E Sea Dragon Takeoff Prep. An HM-14 "Vanguard" MH-53E Sea Dragon helicopter prepares for takeoff from Naval Station Norfolk on a formation training flight on April 13, 2017. (Photograph by MC1 Bill Dodge, courtesy of US Navy.)

HM-14 MH-53E Formation Training Flight. Five HM-14 MH-53E Sea Dragon helicopters leave Naval Station Norfolk on a formation training flight on April 13, 2017. (Photograph by MC1 Bill Dodge, courtesy of US Navy.)

HM-14 MH-53E Takeoff Prep. An HM-14 MH-53E prepares to take off from Naval Station Norfolk on a formation training flight on April 13, 2017. (Photograph by MC3 Jonathan Clay, courtesy of US Navy.)

HSC-28 MH-60S Seahawk Helicopters. HSC-28 "Dragon Whales" sailors perform preflight inspections of their MH-60S Seahawk helicopters at Naval Station Norfolk prior to being assigned to the amphibious assault ship USS *Iwo Jima* (LHD 7) to assist in Hurricane Irma relief operations on September 8, 2017. (Photograph by MC3 Kevin Leitner, courtesy of US Navy.)

On Standby for Hurricane Relief Operations. Sailors and MH-60 Seahawk helicopters belonging to HSC-7 "Dusty Dogs" are on standby at Naval Station Norfolk for Hurricane Florence relief operations on September 15, 2018. (Photograph by MC1 Christopher Lindahl, courtesy of US Navy.)

Welcome Back, HSC-2! An HSC-2 "Fleet Angels" MH-60S Seahawk helicopter returns to Naval Station Norfolk on September 16, 2018, after the passage of Hurricane Florence. (Photograph by K.R. Jackson-Smith, courtesy of US Navy.)

WELCOME BACK, HSC-7! An HSC-7 "Dusty Dogs" MH-60S Seahawk returns to Naval Station Norfolk on September 16, 2018, after the passage of Hurricane Florence. (Photograph by MC1 Christopher Lindahl, courtesy of US Navy.)

Loading Up. Marines of the 22nd Marine Expeditionary Unit board a Naval Station Norfolk–based HM-14 "Vanguard" MH-53E Sea Dragon helicopter aboard the amphibious assault ship USS *Kearsarge* (LHD 3) bound for routine exercises on the East Coast on September 20, 2018. (Photograph by MC3 Michael Eduardo Jorge, courtesy of US Navy.)

A Naval Aviator Reunited with His Children. VRC-40 Lt. Comdr. Benjamin Burnham and his children reunite during the squadron's homecoming at Naval Station Norfolk on December 14, 2018. (Courtesy of US Navy, Video by Mass Communication Specialist 2nd Class Alan Lewis.)

A Navy Family Reunited. Comdr. Pat Morley, HSC-11 "Dragon Slayers" executive officer, reunites with his family during his return to Naval Station Norfolk from a deployment on December 15, 2018. Commander Morley flew MH-60S Seahawk helicopters during his deployment. (Photograph by MC1 Christopher Lindahl, courtesy of US Navy.)

Patrol Squadron (VP) 16 Boeing P-8 Poseidon. Pictured is a VP-16 Boeing P-8 Poseidon at Naval Station Norfolk on July 19, 2019. The Poseidon is the Navy's premier maritime patrol aircraft. VP-16 was hosting midshipmen during professional training at the naval station at the time. (Photograph by Lt. Comdr. Alan Johnson, courtesy of US Navy.)

Advanced E-2D Hawkeye Fleet Service Reception. An advanced E-2D Hawkeye prepares for landing and reception by VAW-120 "Greyhawks" at Naval Station Norfolk on September 9, 2019. The aircraft was the first E-2D, equipped with aerial refueling capability, to enter fleet service. (Photograph by MC3 Nikita Custer, courtesy of US Navy.)

Advanced E-2D Hawkeye Taxi-In. The previously pictured aircraft taxies in following landing at Naval Station Norfolk on September 9, 2019. The aerial refueling probe on the aircraft is clearly visible in this picture. (Photograph by MC3 Nikita Custer, courtesy of US Navy.)

ADVANCED E-2D HAWKEYE TAXI-IN COMPLETION. The E2-D completes its taxi-in following landing at Naval Station Norfolk on September 9, 2019. (Photograph by MC3 Nikita Custer, courtesy of US Navy.)

C-2A Greyhound Fleet Fest Static Display. This C-2A Greyhound was on static display at the Fleet Fest celebration at Naval Station Norfolk on October 19, 2019. (Photograph by MC3 Kody A. Phillips, courtesy of US Navy.)

Bibliography

Hampton Roads Naval Historical Foundation. *Naval Station Norfolk*. Charleston, SC: Arcadia Publishing, 2014.

Yarsinske, Amy Waters. *The Navy Capital of the World: Hampton Roads*. Charleston, SC: The History Press, 2010.

————. *Wings of Valor, Wings of Gold: An Illustrated History of U.S. Naval Aviation*. Stratford, CT: Flying Machines Press, 1998.